# THE ROAD TO EXTINCTION

# IS PAVED IN GOLD

# THE ROAD TO EXTINCTION

## IS PAVED IN GOLD

Ed Amin

# Contents

# THE ROAD TO EXTINCTION

# IS PAVED IN GOLD

Ed Amin

# Chapter 1
# The Reveal

I had a dream, but it was not a dream; it was more like a revelation, but it was not that either. It was divine, heavenly in a way, yet at the same time, it was also logical. You see I finally understood something. And this something was enormous, beyond enormous. If everyone were given this insight, it would change the course of humanity.

It happened in the middle of the night some months ago. It was a night just like any other, nothing out of the ordinary. I went to bed around the same time. Sleep has never been an easy thing. Most times, I struggle with it, often turning on the TV and waiting. But that night, I recall not having this problem. I fell asleep quite easily and slept through the whole night.

At approximately 5AM, I awoke with the most intense, happy feeling I've ever had.

An epiphany had occurred. I had just solved a mystery. But I am not arrogant to believe that I solved this great mystery all on my own. No, in fact, I know that I had absolutely nothing to do with it. I was simply given a gift. I was shown something by someone. The complexity of this thing is not easy to comprehend. In fact, while I was in the middle of this epiphany, I recall having an *aha* moment and understanding **fully** what was being shown to me. At the time, it seemed crystal clear and so simple. I felt an intense happiness that I will never forget.

So, what was I shown? What was this *aha*? Quite simply, it's that we as human beings are all connected to one another. Now my epiphany may not shock you. We've heard that we are all connected, but I quite literally saw it and understood it. I wasn't just being told this—I was shown how we are connected to one another. I was taken step by step through the understanding of this connection. I'm not talking about this in terms of the abstract; we are all quite *physically* connected to each other.

§

Imagine sitting in math class while the teacher is writing an equation on the chalkboard. She begins to explain the equation to you and as she's doing this, you're getting it, actually getting it. It all makes sense. Now, you go home and you open up your math book and in there is the same equation. You stare at it, trying to recall what the math teacher said, but you just can't remember. The problem seems so hard now. Frustration sets in. What happened?

Well, what I was shown during my "vision" was extremely complex, yet as it was shown to me, I understood it. It seemed so simple at the time. The connection we all have to each other is real, undeniable, and on a physical level. Yes, an actual physical connection. That I know with absolute certainty. What I saw were actual physical trails connecting our souls, the core of who we really are with one another. What I can't tell you is the "equation"—*how* we are connected to each other. It was beyond my ability to retain it during the brief period it was shown to me. But I retained the awareness that these connections are in essence absolutely essential to the nucleus of who we are as human beings.

However, this experience was about so much more. It was an awakening. An awakening of our purpose on this planet, the relationships we should all have with each other, how we have lost our way, and how to get back on the right path before it's too late.

§

This by no means will be a spiritual journey. There are many great books on spirituality. Rather, this is about taking a realistic approach to seeing what is truly around us, to what is truly happening, and asking ourselves this question — *why*?

It is also about taking action. No more sitting on the sidelines. No more just accepting what is. As you read this book, you may have internal struggles, moments where you feel challenged, and moments of doubt. But that means you are on the right path. It means you are looking beyond yourself. It means you care about saving humanity. I invite you to discover a new way of thinking.

# Chapter 2
# Compete, Adapt or Die

We live in a world where our existence is based on competition: a world of continuous strife and struggle. But this constant struggle of survival is self-imposed. We've created this system all on our own, but this system is barbaric.

At the beginning of our existence, it was a constant struggle just to survive by learning how to utilize the resources this planet has to offer. Resources can be defined as anything we universally need to live (food, water, shelter, etc.). So man figured out that it was a lot easier to fight other men to take what was not his.

Thus, humanity's motto became "Might makes right." If you were strong, then you were right. After all, there would be no one left to challenge you. You could write history any way you wanted. And throughout our history, that is what men have done. Man would form groups of men called armies, of which one would be the aggressor and the other the defender. Think of all the battles that have been fought in Eurasia, Africa, and throughout the world.

As mankind continued his pursuit of wars, what was once based on capturing those resources took a backseat to something more ominous, *the unquenchable desire to conquer.* Yes, resources were still important, but war quickly became more about pride, honor, ideology, and proving one's self. This need, this desire, satisfied one very important thing in man, the ego. That is, man's sense of self-importance. War, at times, became about ego, with the real tangible benefit of resources being a secondary objective.

Over time, it became accepted that just because that is what we have done in the past, somehow this defines who we are now. That this way of being, ego-driven, needs to be accepted. That is what bad people have always been telling good people:

*"You are too gullible, too naive, and too nice. You should just sit back and let us do all the work. We know how to get things, and get things done. We're the big boys. Our*

*civilization is rooted in evil, in hatred, destruction, killing, stealing, competing, and fighting. That's just the way it is. Accept it. And if you are to survive, you must be this way too, or align with those who are."*

§

But if other worlds exist beyond our own in this vast universe, and those species are watching us, they would probably see us as atrocious creatures. Moreover, not just atrocious creatures, but creatures without logic, creatures that don't make sense. Our human history doesn't make sense especially given all the resources that this planet has to offer. With all of the growing technology and automation that we now possess, we have the potential to render what we once were a thing of the past. We have the ability, with very little effort, with very little labor (thanks to machinery and ingenuity), to feed and shelter every single person on this planet. **We no longer need to fight over resources.** *So, why do we?*

§

Why do we let people starve, sleep in the street, go without medicine, or endure pain? Why do we get some perverse satisfaction when we do better than others or when we see others fail? The greatest enemy man faces is not from other countries, not from space, but from deep within ourselves. Ego has been at the heart of every major decision made throughout history. It has played a vital role in the deaths of hundreds of millions of people. It controls us every day. We give way to it very easily, unable or unwilling to see its existence, its hold on us, yet we can somehow see it in others.

The prevailing thought in our society is that life is all about self-responsibility; that we are each responsible for ourselves and not for others.

*If you can't make it in this world, then that's your fault. I have no obligation to assist you in any way. If I make billions of dollars, why in the hell would I share that with anyone? I will make my charitable donation because it makes me look good and it serves as a tax deduction. I will attend my congregation on Sunday, pretending that I care about the plight of man, but forget all about it from Monday to Friday. I am after all, a hypocrite, but I have an ego that fortunately won't let me see it and that hungers to be satisfied.*

## A New Breed of Man

When Darwin borrowed the phrase "survival of the fittest" in talking about his theory on natural selection, he was referring to the physical or biochemical form. That is, the survival of a species is predicated on how that species can physically adapt to its environment to better reproduce.

As such, when we look around this planet we see that life is continually adapting. Take Tardigrades for example. Tardigrades are water-dwelling, eight-legged, micro-animals. They are known for being one of the most resilient organisms found. They can withstand extreme temperatures from -458F to 300F or pressures six times greater than those found in the deepest ocean trenches or even radiation hundreds of times higher than the lethal dose for humans. They can even go without food or water for more than 30 years. Such creatures don't become this way unless there was a need in order to survive. In Darwin's natural selection theory, a species "selects for" characteristics that enhance its chances of reproduction and therefore survival. These adaptations alter our genes and are passed onto future generations. This means that over time, our genetic makeup is changing. But what does that mean now—in our society—as it relates to man? What are we selecting for?

Unlike the beginnings of humankind, survival is no longer about being physically the strongest to guarantee reproduction. In most cultures, it's no longer about hunting and catching one's food, physically fighting off competitors or seeking resources in the natural environment.

Rather, in most human cultures today, survival is about non-physical characteristics: who can lie the best, manipulate the best, steal the best, or deceive the best, to get the most money to buy the resources needed. So, the question of natural selection now becomes—what are we breeding? **What exactly are we developing and turning into?**

§

Competition plays a vital role in this selection process and suggests in theory that a species that is less suited to its environment will either adapt or die.

So, it would seem that if our species were selecting for such traits as lying, deceiving, manipulating, etc., then it would stand to reason that those not having such traits (those that are nice) will find themselves on the road to extinction.

§

In our current environment, it appears that "nice" no longer has a place in our world or at the very least is decreasing considerably. And while there are still nice people, lots and lots of nice people, there is an ever-shrinking space for them to live and work. There are, of course, nice people out there who are successful, who got ahead without hurting others or giving up their souls. But unless you believe that everyone who is successful is nice, caring, or compassionate, we need to examine those that are not nice. Because based on the current state of the world, a conversation is warranted on those individuals.

## The Red Fox Experiment

Is there some evidence out there that can show that temperament traits can indeed be altered/changed in a species?

In 1959 the Soviet Union started an experiment known as the Russian Domesticated Red Fox Experiment. The experiment aimed to see whether a red fox, through selective breeding, could become tamer and more dog-like in its behavior.

In an article by Lyudmila N. Trut in American Scientist Magazine (March-April 1999 issue) on the experiment, Trut writes, "The least domesticated foxes, those that flee from experimenters or bite when stroked or handled, are assigned to Class III … Foxes in Class II let themselves be petted and handled but show no emotionally friendly response to experimenters. Foxes in Class I are friendly toward experimenters, wagging their tails and whining."

Trut noted that by the sixth generation in the experiment, the researchers had to add an even higher-scoring category of tameness. She stated, "Members of Class IE, the 'domesticated Elite' are eager to establish human contact, whimpering to attract attention and sniffing and licking experimenters like dogs." Within 10 generations, 18 percent of fox pups were elite. Today, elite foxes makeup 70 to 80 percent of their population.[1]

The result was that Russian scientists now had domesticated foxes that are "fundamentally different in temperament and behavior from their wild forebears." It should be noted that the researchers kept a control group of the "aggressive strain" to preserve the wild-type behaviors.

In an article published in Current Biology (Nov 2005) about the genetic differences between the two fox populations, 40 genes were found to be different between the domesticated and non-domesticated farm-raised foxes. And around 2,700 genes differed between the wild foxes and the farm-raised foxes.[2]

This experiment demonstrates that in just 10 generations, scientists literally removed the aggressive genes from a fox, and therefore potentially out of an entire species. That is, it is possible to fundamentally change the temperament of a species.

§

## Selecting for Behavior

If it's possible within only 10 generations to produce a kinder, gentler, more loving fox, is it not possible to produce the same effect in humans, only in the opposite direction and without selective breeding?

This experiment suggests that our behavior, like the foxes, may adapt over time. That we may select for psychological characteristics. So, while our ancestors selected for physical prowess, what if we are now selecting for psychological prowess?

In our ancestor's time, those in power used to be those who were physically the strongest or the best reproducers. However, those in power now are those with the best psychological traits to gain power and wealth: key aggressive temperament traits such as a huge ego, lack of compassion, selfishness, lack of empathy, cunningness, and deception.

So, if generation after generation of the wealthy and powerful produce offspring with similar psychological makeup, won't we end up with individuals in power who have those traits? Is it not conceivable that such traits could be passed onto their offspring, and their offspring, and down the line? Is it not possible then that power (those who have the ability to affect the lives of so many people) will be in the hands of the "aggressive strain" of humans? What if this has already happened or beginning to happen?

What I am proposing here is this: the way you think, what you think and what you believe, has a direct link on your physiology, specifically shaping and altering your genes. Affecting who you are and what your offspring will be like. Altering your soul and your children's souls.

§

And when generations after generation are exposed to horrific stimuli or suffer in poverty, our natural genetic instincts may be to adapt behaviorally, and with that may come the loss of compassion, sensitivity, and caring.

What of the nice people, those with traits such as kindness and empathy, who want to help their fellow man? Won't those traits be selected out?

And of those nice people who do survive, environmental factors such as growing up in poverty, seeing horrors portrayed on television or in everyday life alters or possibly mutates those caring, nice genes. This process wouldn't occur over one generation, but if similar conditions existed in one generation after the next, then by a certain point, those traits would be completely altered, perhaps even gone completely.

## Good or Bad

Some may argue that natural selection is a good thing; after all, it has the word "natural" in it. And we all know that anything that is natural or deals with nature is good for you. Others may say if natural selection dictates that the strong survive and the weak perish, then that's the way it should be. I would argue however that given where we are now in human history, that it's a bad thing; an extremely awful thing. The reason is that we've put ourselves (as a species) on this road where psychological natural selection is taking place. So now natural selection is selecting for those with power and all the other aggressive traits that I've mentioned before.

Since we are thinking, self-aware beings, we had a choice and still do. Natural selection however does not. It only looks at one variable in its operation—survival. That is the only thing natural selection cares about. It doesn't see or understand anything else. It doesn't know whether there is an afterlife. It's not concerned with whether you have a soul or not. It only understands one thing—surviving. So it treats us no differently than any other animal.

Being self-aware is the only thing that we have that distinguishes us from other animals and gives us a chance to change our path.

## The Shock Factor

Our human history is filled with a multitude of events which have taken place that have truly shocked us. Take for example the assassination of John F Kennedy on November 22, 1963. The news was so horrific that you could find people openly crying in the streets. It was rare to find anyone, even around the world, that didn't truly feel a sense of sadness or sorrow. Ask anyone living at that time "Where were you when you heard of the JFK assassination" and they can tell you immediately. In present times however, in American society, there appears to be a sense that not much can shock us anymore. Is it that the events in modern times that we are witnessing are less horrific? I don't think so. I believe that our reactions to horrific events are changing.

What happens when you expose people to bad news every day from the day they're born to the day they die? To poverty, murders, beheadings, terrorism, etc. To lots and lots of horrifying visual images that weren't around during your great-grandparent's time? What sort of adaptation is taking place? Are you that same person that you once were when you were a child and still carried your innocence? Or have you become desensitized to the horrors that exist in order to manage living? Have you become meaner, calloused, cold-hearted, and unsympathetic because your survival now depends on you becoming this way?

Do you think that by being exposed to these horrors portrayed every day on television, in the news, on the Internet, in print or in everyday life, that you are somehow being changed? That our brain chemistry and genes are being altered? Somehow being adapted in an effort to survive our environment; much like Tardigrades or other organisms that had to endure living in harsh environments. If we as humans are subject to the same laws of nature as every other creature, then the answer is yes. I believe that as a natural process, we are changing and that we are passing these physiological changes onto our offspring.

§

Is it conceivable that just like the red fox experiment, our genes could also be changing? I believe the answer is yes. I believe that our body's chemistry, our genes, are mutating to better cope with our environmental surroundings. And these changes are not for the good, but for the bad. I believe that our very souls are invariably being altered, perhaps even being killed off. As a result, what we were once is not who we are now, nor who we will be in the future. Place any living thing in a hostile environment and what do you see? It either adapts or it dies.

Through evolution and survival of the fittest, our gene pool will evolve to become angrier, more self-centered, more of an atrocious creature. That is the road we are currently on. If we should happen to exist in a few hundred years, what will we be? Will we be one step closer to God: that is, kinder, gentler, more loving and peaceful people? Or will we be one step closer to the Devil—hideous monsters that care about nothing but our own survival, in which killing will become a way of life, in which we will look back on our ancestors smirking and declaring them fools for being nice and caring about their fellow man.

As our brain chemistry, our genes, our very souls are changing, we will find ourselves one step closer to the Devil rather than one step closer to God. As earth slowly becomes hell, there will be no going back. Are we comfortable with aligning ourselves with that of evil in order to survive on this planet? Are we comfortable with our souls forever being altered, perhaps even being killed off?

§

The phenomenal thing is that this is not all happening by mere coincidence. There is an intentional driving force behind all of it!

# Chapter 3
# Ego

The first sin in the universe was **pride** and the first being to sin was Lucifer. Lucifer was an angel, one of God's angels, but that is not what Lucifer wanted. In Isaiah 14:13, Lucifer tells us what he wanted, "I will ascend to heaven; I will raise my throne above the stars of God; I will sit on the mount of assembly on the heights of Zaphon; I will ascend to the tops of the clouds; I will make myself like the Most High." What Lucifer wanted was to take over heaven, to be God.

Is there a difference between ego and pride? In the terms used here and more so in religious passages, the answer would be no. There is no relevant distinction between the two. They are for all practical purposes one and the same.

While we as humans have the ability to be self-aware, are we always aware of when we are being awful? I believe that we are able to—at the very least—glimpse at ourselves and at times notice when our behavior or our actions are bad. Unlike other animals, we can be self-aware, but we also have something no other creature has to help us be the atrocious creatures we are. We have the ego. Ego serves to help us justify anything in life. You want to commit mass murder, ego will help you with that. You want to cheat on your taxes or your partner, there's ego, your best friend, talking you through it.

The idea of good and bad goes hand in hand with ego. And so, the concept of a God and a Devil must also go hand in hand. We know that as human beings, we have among us people who are good and people who are bad. Therefore, the concept of good and bad exists to us in our universe.

If we were to apply a little reasoning to religion, I would say it's completely logical that God, upon discovering one of his angels as bad, should cast him out rather than kill him. After all, God has the power to do so.[3]

Now, had God chosen to kill Lucifer and therefore eliminate evil, then evil would never have come to his sons and daughters now living on this planet. But then what of God? In doing so, God would have ceased to be good. Even now, with God witnessing all the horrors that his angel has caused, He cannot kill him.

I understand that. You can never defeat evil by killing it, because by doing so, by that very action, you become evil yourself. So it seems to me that God did the only thing he could do, which was cast him out.

One way I have found to live among evil, that is, the evil that resides within you (our ego), is to live as two distinct individuals inside your one body: one as yourself and the second as a watcher of the self. The watcher (our conscience) lives outside our physical form and observes us as we go about our day, as we think, and as we talk, with the sole purpose of monitoring our ego. The watcher dutifully jumps in when the ego wants to speak or act and does its very best to keep the ego under control. By doing that, the watcher will try to keep our souls pure making it harder for the devil to have complete control or influence over us. In doing so, we will then be one step closer to God, as I do not believe God has an ego.

This is something we desire; to be held by God in his loving arms; to feel safe and loved. Don't we all want that?

Perhaps the truth is that we are never destined to defeat evil in this world. Maybe it is a fundamental law like the existence of gravity. But if there is a chance to defeat evil, we need to do some things that are very important. The first of which is to become more self-aware, to listen to the watcher (our conscience) so that we may better control the ego.

§

# Chapter 4
# Money: The Myths, the Programming, the Means to Control Others

**We no longer need to fight over resources.** *So why do we?* The superficial answer to this question is of course money. It rules, controls, dominates just about everyone living on this planet. It has a stronger hold on some, not so much on others. It is on our minds constantly. It makes us greedy, callous, and arrogant. We fight over it; some will happily stab their mother, brother, and friends in the back for it. We'll consider doing just about anything for it. We'll lie, steal, and cheat. Our principles go right out the door when it comes to money.

## A World Made from Gold

Let's take a step back and look at the absurdity of our financial system and how it all started. To do so, we need a general understanding of our planet. Our planet is made up of just 98 elements. Everything you see, hear, and touch is made up of those 98 elements. Hard to believe, isn't it? In this great big planet of ours, there are only 98 components that make up our world.

For example, diamonds are composed of just one element, carbon. The walls in your home are made of the mineral gypsum. Gypsum is composed of several elements found on the list of those 98 elements. What about Gold? Gold is also an element on that list. It's also considered a mineral. While some minerals (for example Topaz) can be made up of several elements, gold is not. Gold contains only one element called Gold (Au).

Now, at some point throughout our human history, men decided that they were going to pick one of these 98 elements and make it valuable. This idea caught on. Consider the notion of the entire world deciding that some hard to find mineral (gold) is going to be worth something to everyone—not just to some people in some parts of the world, but to everyone in every part of the world. Without everyone participating, this scheme would never work. It required the cooperation of everyone. How else would you be able to sell your salt, for example, that you've labored to mine that serves a real purpose of preserving meat for nuggets of a shiny yellow object, if you couldn't turn around and use those same shiny objects to buy a cow with?

Gold, for the most part, has no functional or practical purpose. It's very soft, not the best conductor of electricity, and you can't do much with it even if you mix it with other elements. Iron for instance has more uses. And what do we do with gold when we find it? We store it. We build repositories most likely made of iron (steel) to protect the gold. Gold is never really *consumed*. You can't use it up. Iron on the other hand rusts. But gold found thousands of years ago is still pretty much the same as it was then.

So why was gold chosen? The answer is very simple. **The notion of using something rare and hard to find is designed purposefully as an exclusionary means to restrict resources from the masses. Let me repeat that in a different way: by using something rare and hard to find, you get to control the resources that are available on this planet from the people that need it.**

**Translated a third way, you now have the ability to control people, because if a person wants to survive and feed his family, he has to do what you want him to do.**

§

Gold became a currency that was widely accepted no matter where you were in the world. Even governments used gold to purchase things. But over time, there was a shift away from gold to paper money. Then there was a shift from paper currency that was backed by gold to currency that was backed by the credibility of the government issuing it. The reason for this is very simple. As a country's economy grew, the government could not possibly have enough gold on hand to satisfy redemptions if all the paper money being circulated were cashed in for gold.

So, on a basic primitive level, you could say that the world's financial system started out by trading rocks (nuggets of gold) found on our planet; rocks that serve no purpose other than as a decoration on one's body. It might sound like I'm talking about cavemen, but this was as recent as only a couple of hundred years ago in American history and it's what formed the basis for the world economy we have now.

Ninety-eight naturally occurring elements make up our planet, and one element is chosen to be used as currency.

§

## Gold — The Currency of Judgment

Armed with this idiotic concept, we now have the means to set up classes with those who have gold being of higher class than those who don't. Think about that for a minute. With absolutely no difference between you and another person; after all you both are made of flesh and bones, you both go to the bathroom in the same way; yet you are somehow relegated to being inferior solely based on gold, or money.

What you think of yourself, what others think of you, and how you are treated in this world is solely based on how much of this one element you have in your possession. Your entire self-worth, whether you see yourself as having value or not and whether others see you as having value or not, is all based on this one thing.

Based on that fact and that fact alone, we as a society could now assign a value to a person's innate worth as a human being by how much of this element they have. Whether we realize it or not, we have been programmed to see this as well. We look at a homeless person far differently than say a doctor.

And we have developed all sorts of excuses why that is acceptable. *"Well a doctor went to school and helps the sick,"* is something you might say. On a practical level, you would be right. But on a human level, what makes them different? The answer is, of course they're not.

When you heard the word "doctor" or the word "homeless," you presupposed many things about each person. In the case of the homeless man, many people would pass judgments on this person without knowing anything about him. How many people see a homeless person and think *"alcoholic, no job, lazy, no education"* and so on? Let's say you thought these things, and it turns out you are right about all of them.

Do you now feel empowered to pass judgment? To say that it's his fault for the condition that he's in?

If you did, I would say that you are mistaken. And the reason is that there are thousands of variables that contributed and led to where this man is today; variables such as his genes, his brain chemistry, his childhood, the time in which he existed on this planet, the place in which he existed on this planet, who his parents were, his IQ, etc. Change just one of those variables—variables by the way that he had no control over, and this homeless person could very well not have been homeless, but perhaps that doctor that we are comparing him to.

Admiring someone just because they achieved something on this earth is without a doubt ego-driven. It is not pure because it is not about the true person. It's about "stuff" that's relevant only to this world.

What is pure then, you might ask? What is one thing, the only thing that could be applied to this world and the next? To a world of tangibles and a world of intangibles; a world where our existence is energy. The answer is quite simple. It's your soul. It's the true essence of who you are.

But mankind has decided that if a person does not have money, then civilization has the right to deprive that person of the right to exist. Take starving children in third-world countries. No money, they starve and then they die. It's that simple.

§

## The Declining Value of Money

If it were a true universal law that our existence should be rooted in money—that we should define ourselves based on money, that if indeed it is what God wants (as some wealthy individuals would have us believe), then God would have made money a requirement to enter the gates of heaven. At the very least, God would allow you to take all the money that you have into the afterlife. But to those wealthy individuals, sadly that is not so. All that money you have will sit idly by in your bank account while you pass into the next life without it.

To those struggling financially, I can tell you with absolute certainty that this accumulation of money by the wealthy and by big companies, will soon result in money becoming meaningless. It will, in fact, just be paper. And all those individuals hoarding it will find themselves no better than anyone else.

The reason for this is that fewer and fewer people will have money. It will become greatly concentrated among a few. The greed that accompanies money will see to it that human nature, as it exists now, keeps money contained and hoarded among a small number of people. There will reach a point when companies have so much money that money itself will begin to lose its value.

Imagine walking along the beach with the hope and desire to find a seashell. As you walk, you notice a shiny beautiful object. You pick it up and find that it's the beautiful seashell you've been looking for. You admire it and put it in your bag to take home. As you continue your walk, you turn the corner and behind a huge rock, the beach continues for miles.

As you look outward, the beach is covered with millions upon billions of seashells, piled five feet high. You pick one up and pull out the seashell you've just put in your bag to compare them. You find that it's an exact match. In fact, all the seashells are identical. This one seashell that you admired and thought was special is no longer special.

When companies end up with oodles and oodles of money that they no longer know what to do with, it will become just a pile of paper. And when more and more people have less or none of this exchangeable material, they will end up dropping out of the system.

As the number of people participating in this exchange system begins to dwindle, the amount of currency these individuals have begins to accumulate. Eventually, the number of participants shrinks to such a small level and the currency of the wealthy becomes so vast, that it no longer means anything or has any value.

Think of it like the game Monopoly. When there is a winner, when there is just one person left that has all the money, how valuable is that money to the person who is out of the game? Or even how valuable is that money to the winner who now has no one to play with?

# Chapter 5
# Population Growth, the Shocking Truth

Are you sitting down? Here is a shocking fact: currently, we're adding approximately 1 billion people to our planet every 10-15 years. That's one Billion with a capital "B."

§

In the year 1000, it was estimated that world population was approximately 300 million. The world population did not reach 1 billion until approximately 1850. It took 850 years to grow the population by 700 million. However, from 1850 to the present, the world population grew by **6.5 billion**. So, in a short span of 165 years, we've added approximately 6.5 billion to our current level of 7.7 billion. And there is no end in sight.

We can keep expecting growth of an additional one billion people every 15 years and continuing at that rate. Can anyone fathom a billion anything? I have a hard time comprehending what a billion is. I can maybe understand what a million is: a million people. Maybe I can even comprehend what 10 million is.

New York City with its five boroughs has a population of 8.5 million. Manhattan has a population of 1.7 million. Los Angeles has a population of approximately 4 million. So how can I try and understand what 100 million is, let alone 1 billion people newly inhabiting our planet every 10—15 years?

§

Why is it that we don't see the prime-time news channels covering this? No one dares talk about this staggering population growth for a few reasons. One reason is that it's somehow seen as a personal choice. Another, is that from a religious perspective, it's also seen as somehow sacred, a blessing, a gift. And finally, and most importantly, it's financial.

Population growth contributes to financial growth. More mouths to feed, people to clothe, house, send to college, buy lots of gadgets, cars, oil, etc.

No one is talking about it and only a few government entities are calling on people to curtail this growth.

Why? Very simply, it's all about money. We are a consumer-driven economy. Value is derived from someone consuming something, whether that is goods or services. More people translate into more consumers.

What are the consequences of an over-populated planet? With population growth comes overcrowding, and that leads to many issues: violence, anger, crime, and competition. Resources will become scarce; there will be greater competition for everything. It will become an us versus them situation.

§

Another consequence is anger. Take for example something as simple and as ordinary as driving into work during rush hour. The negative feelings that come over people every day as they crawl at a snail's pace day in and day out. How about having to wait to get a seat at a restaurant or driving to the beach and not being able to find a parking spot?

The toll of all this negativity has an impact upon your psyche. It has to. Just like it would have a positive impact on you if you could drive to work without any traffic, enjoying a smooth, beautiful ride or going to a restaurant and getting seated right away at their best table or going to the beach and finding parking abundantly available would have a positive impact on you.

Anger, bitterness and hatred is forever changing our humanity. What we are, what it means to be human beings is slowly, no not slowly, is quickly being replaced by our barbaric nature to kill, destroy, and do whatever it takes to survive. There is a lack of true self-awareness, of what our purpose is and of what is to follow after this life.

How did we become such despicable creatures? Ones that could care less about anyone including the homeless and the elderly. How is it that such a large percentage of the population in our society feels this way? You hear things like, *"Let them fend for themselves. It's their tough luck that they weren't so smart and made money. The world would be better off if they simply died or got shipped somewhere else."* All because these people don't possess the one thing that they have—money.

One of the reasons I believe there seems to be a growing population of individuals who feel this way is precisely because of population growth. The number of bad people as a percentage of the population is growing, while the population of good people is shrinking.

Please know that when I call us atrocious or despicable creatures, I am not talking about you as an individual. I am talking about us as a group, as a collection of people. Whether you like it or not, you and I belong to this group (the human race). And the history of our civilization, of monsters like Hitler and Stalin, are part of who we are. We all have to own it.

These wealthy individuals never stop to think that humanity would likely be better off if they didn't exist. That kindness and compassion would be more apparent and handed down to the next generation, not the hatred, bitterness, greed, superficiality, cunningness, disingenuous, selfishness, uncaringness that resides within them.

But it's not just about the planet and how we are destroying it, it's also about human beings and how we are changing from being a compassionate, kind, and loving souls to a greedy, selfish, and uncaring species.

Lives tend to become devalued when you have overpopulation. It's a natural course when you have so many people living on this planet all vying for the same things. Is this what we want to be, because from here the picture continues to get more grim.

§

# Chapter 6
# The Last Line of Defense Destroyed by the Wealthy and Powerful

*There is more crime, more violence, more terrorism, more of everything that is bad. And law enforcement has to prioritize.* At least that's the perception you get when watching and reading the news. The fact is bad people are exploiting the lack of funding that governments are giving to our law enforcement.

Look around you. Turn on the news. Shootings, bombings, terrorism, murders, genocide, and war is everywhere. You may say *"Come on now, we've had this going on since the beginning of time."* And for the sake of argument, I will agree with you. But something else is happening that is new and that is our reaction to the horrors. The feelings we have now when we hear about these acts of violence is not the same feelings our grandparents had many years ago. And the actions we take when we learn of these events are not the same as our grandparents. Therefore, the actions taken by our governments, by our law enforcement entities, are not the same as it used to be.

Law enforcement has served a gigantic role in our society beyond just capturing the bad guys. They are the front line, the gatekeepers that keep evil from permeating our society. They held the line of what was good and bad and their role in society has been greatly undervalued.

Religion, no matter which faith, has a practical aspect. And that is that religion sought to keep man from doing bad. In that regard, religion could be thought of as a proactive approach to prevent bad acts from occurring, whatever that act is. But when man falters and commits an act against their fellow man, against the society in which they live, then law enforcement would step in and keep that bad, that evil, at bay.

Law enforcement protected our society by seeking to keep evil out of our daily lives; and when it did enter, by not allowing it to flourish. Think about a world where law enforcement does not exist, where evil roams freely. It's terrifying to think about, isn't it? These gatekeepers serve not just to protect you and I, but also to guard the very essence of who we are, our very hearts and souls, our humanity.

§

## Historical Truths about Crime

According to a Gallup Poll conducted in 2015, and again in 2016, 70% of Americans believe that crime is on the rise. This perception that Americans have about crime is often disputed by politicians and the media citing data showing crime is on the decline. They will argue that this perception that Americans have that crime is on the rise is simply false.

So, what is the real story? Is crime on the decline as the media and some politicians would have us believe? The short answer is no. Historical data shows that crime is on the rise.

What politicians and the media tend to do if they want to show that crime is on the decline, is to pick a year, usually around 1991 (highest crime rate year in U.S. history) as their starting year for comparison. They will then compare that starting year to present day and say, *"see, crime is on the decline."*

This is, of course, nonsense.

For an accurate, historical representation of whether crime is on the rise or not in our society, you must go back at least 50 years. After all, we are talking about society's behavior from a historical perspective in the United States. Simply picking a year in U.S. history when crime was at its highest to make a point that crime is on the decline, is playing fast-and-loose with the truth.

In 1961, J. Edgar Hoover, then Director of the Federal Bureau of Investigation (FBI) published the annual Uniform Crime Reports (UCR) for the United States for the year 1960. In 1960 there were 9,136 killings (murder and nonnegligent manslaughter). In 2015, the FBI shows that number to be 15,696, an increase of over 70%. In 1960, there were 15,555 rapes. In 2015 that number rose to 90,185 (excludes revised definition of rape). That is an increase of nearly 500%.

With regard to total crime, that is all violent and property crime, in 1960 the total offenses were

1,861,281. In 2015, that number is 9,191,335, an increase of almost 400%.

Table 1 shows the actual numbers as published by the FBI.

§

The Road To Extinction Is Paved In Gold

Table 1: National crime then and now.[4*]

| Year | Total Crime | Total Violent Crime | Total Property Crime | Murder | Rape (Legacy Definition) | Robbery | Aggravated Assault | Burglary | Larceny | Auto Theft |
|---|---|---|---|---|---|---|---|---|---|---|
| 1949** | 1,758,410 | 161,350 | 1,597,060 | 6,990 | 16,380 | 59,120 | 78,860 | 409,400 | 1,024,520 | 163,140 |
| 1960*** | 1,861,261 | 243,891 | 1,617,370 | 9,136 | 15,555 | 88,970 | 130,230 | 821,057 | 474,911 | 321,402 |
| 2015**** | 9,191,335 | 1,197,704 | 7,993,631 | 15,696 | 90,185 | 327,374 | 764,449 | 1,579,527 | 5,706,346 | 707,758 |
| Increase from 1960 to 2015 | 7,330,074 | 953,813 | 6,376,261 | 6,560 | 74,630 | 238,404 | 634,219 | 758,470 | 5,231,435 | 386,356 |
| Percent Increase from 1960 to 2015 | 394% | 391% | 394% | 72% | 480% | 268% | 487% | 92% | 1102% | 120% |

* UCR program is voluntary meaning that it's up to local jurisdictions to report crime in their area and some states do not have State UCR Programs. Therefore the data represented in Table 1 should be considered as being underreported.

** Prior to 1958, data was not imputed.

*** Data obtained from the original UCR FBI report published in July 1961.

**** Total Crime and Total Violent Crime excludes the figures for the new definition of rape in order to provide an accurate historical comparison.

56

For a historical perspective, I have also included the data for 1949. I chose 1949 and 1960 as the data was readily available, but I could have chosen any year back then and the results would have been the same.

Facts are facts and they do not lie. Historically, crime is not on the decline, quite the opposite. However, professionals employ a unique trick when they want to show that crime is on the decline. It's called the "Crime Rate." The crime rate factors in population size for any given year. So, if you're looking at crime as a rate per 100,000 inhabitants, then you can make the case that the rate of say murder 5.1 in 1960 was higher than 4.9 in 2015. Even though there were more murders in 2015 than in 1960, you could say that the *"crime rate went down."*

When you see a murder rate of 4.9 for example in 2015, what that means is that for every 100,000 people living in this country, 5 (4.9) of them were murdered. Or when the crime rate for rape in 2015 is 38.6, that means that for every 100,000 people, 38 were raped. In the case of rape however, that rate seems to be underreported. Since the vast majority of rapes tend to be towards women and since half the United States population are women, the crime rate for rape would actually be double the current figure, approximately

76. That means that for every 100,000 **women** living in this country, 76 have been raped.

By using the "rate," you have a way of masking or hiding the increase in the actual number of crimes by indexing it to the increase in population growth. In fact, there is a slew of articles that try to do just that: *"U.S. Homicide Rate at a 51-Year Low"*, *"Crime Rates Have Fallen Since the Early 1990s"*, *"Murder Rate Drops to 33-Year Low."* If you notice that in all these articles and many more, the word "rate" is used.

Should society just accept that the number of murders, rapes, theft, etc., will continue to increase just because population is increasing?

Will there ever be an actual number to which we will say, "Enough is enough?" That this number is too high and unacceptable or will it always be based on the size of our population?

It is preposterous to justify an increase in crime by basically saying, *"Well our population increased, so we are naturally going to have more murders, rapes and theft."*

At what point will the actual numbers themselves become unacceptable? Will 20,000 murders, 30,000 murders, 150,000 rapes, 200,000 rapes be the numbers to prompt further resources? What about non-violent crimes, currently at 8 million. What is the magic number there to get government to act?

Citizens are right to say that crime is increasing because it is. In their town or city, in that space in which they live and work, there is more crime. Just because there are more people living there doesn't take away from the actual number of murders, rapes, and theft.

When the FBI and law enforcement professionals use population size (demographic) to calculate the "crime rate," my response is "Ok, but what about geographic?" Why is geographic data excluded from the calculations?

Did the geography of the region (town, city, county, state) in which those murders or crime took place change? Did the United States grow in size from 1960 to 2015 (Hawaii was the last state admitted in August 1959)? Did the city, town or area in which you live grow in size in terms of land (space). The answer is no. The same boundaries that define your town or city then are still the same now. And in that same space of land in which you live, you had an increase in crime. That is a fact.

If I live in Michigan for example, a state with defined boundary lines and there are 2,099,382 more people living there now than in 1960, what difference does it make to me what the rate of crime per 100,000 inhabitants are? There are hundreds more murders, thousands of more rapes and tens of thousands more assaults in the same space in which I live.

§

Think of yourself living in a fish tank. In that fish tank, there's 10 fish including you. Now within a year, one of those fish eats another fish. Could be you but maybe not. Let's say you manage to survive to next year, great.

Next year comes and the owner puts in 41 more fish so now there are 50 fish living in the same fish tank with you. Now this year, 5 fish get eaten by other fish.

To the FBI, the professionals and the media, they would tell you that the "crime rate" is the same for both years (1 per 10 fish); you have a one out of 10 chance that you will be eaten. Or if in that last year, 4 fish were eaten instead of 5, they would tell you that the "crime rate" has gone down. They would tell you that you are wrong to think that crime is increasing.

Now substitute the word "eaten" for murder, rape, aggravated assault, burglary, etc.

The government using "crime rate" as measure is tantamount to it asking its citizens to play the odds as if we were in a casino: that your life is a probability, a statistic. Sounds comforting, doesn't it? Ignoring or trying to minimize (downplay) the fact that there are more murders, more rapes, more violent crime now than in the past by using "crime rate" is deception plain and simple. And more so, it's an outright lie to say that historically crime has gone down.

§

That is how the government and the media want us to think about crime. Instead of focusing on reducing the number of murders and rapes, they rely on population growth as a way to mask the true numbers.

Keep in mind that the figures displayed here are numbers per year. Extrapolating these numbers over the last twenty, fifty years, and you're talking about murders in the hundreds of thousands and rapes in the millions.

§

There are two other points of significance worth mentioning. According to the National Crime Victimization Survey (NCVS) conducted for the period 2006-2010 by the U.S. Department of Justice, it found that 52% or 3,382,200 **annually** of all **violent** victimizations were not reported. For non-violent crime, 60% or 10,547,200 **annually** were not reported.[5] What that means is the data reported by the FBI and shown in table 1 is **significantly** underreported.

§

The other point from this study is that of those victims in 2010 who did not report the violent crime, 20% did not do so because they believed that the police **"would not or could not help."** This is up from 7% in 1994.

All of this confirms one thing; crime is on the rise. This nonsense that professionals are using to justify current conditions such as using rates per 100,000 people or comparing current numbers to 20-30 years ago needs to stop.

§

## Where Are They?

There's good news for murderers. Statistically speaking, based on national data, if you were to commit murder, there's a 40% chance that you will not be arrested for the crime. We are not even talking about prosecution and conviction. All we are talking about is law enforcement doing their job, discovering who committed the crime and making an arrest.

The FBI not only keeps track of crimes committed, but it also keeps track of crimes cleared by arrest. If the police arrest someone, charge that person with the commission of the offense and turns that person over to the court for prosecution, then that would be considered as the police having cleared a crime.

Law enforcement can also clear a crime by exceptional means as well. For example, if the police confront someone they believe to be the offender of a crime, and that offender puts up a fight that results in their death, that original crime would be considered cleared.

According to Uniform Crime Reports prepared by the FBI, law enforcement agencies throughout the country in 1960 cleared 92.3% of murders, 72.5% of rape, and 29.5% of burglary.

In 2015 law enforcement agencies cleared 61.5% of murders, 37.8% of rape, and 12.9% of burglary.

Table 2 shows just how effectively law enforcement is doing their job.

§

Table 2: Crime cleared by arrest and exceptional means. [6]

| Year | Murder Cleared | Rape Cleared | Robbery Cleared | Aggravated Assault Cleared | Burglary Cleared | Larceny Cleared | Auto Theft Cleared |
|------|------|------|------|------|------|------|------|
| 1949 | 93.7% | 80.2% | 39.5% | 77.2% | 29.0% | 21.6% | 27.3% |
| 1960 | 92.3% | 72.5% | 38.5% | 75.8% | 29.5% | 20.1% | 25.7% |
| 2015 | 61.5% | 37.8% | 29.3% | 54.0% | 12.9% | 21.9% | 13.1% |

Law enforcement agencies have a dual role in society. The first is considered proactive—that is to deter crime from happening in the first place. The fact that crime has risen from fifty years ago, shows that they have failed in that regard.

§

The second role is to apprehend those who have committed crimes in order to have them removed from society or punished in some way as a form of deterrence from future behavior. The statistics showing the number of cases cleared by law enforcement agencies is abysmal to say the least and represents a significant drop from 1960.

§

With the development of forensic science over the last fifty years such as DNA, computer databases, as well as cameras on street corners, in restaurants, etc., you would think that arrests (clearance percentage) would go up.

So where are our police, our law enforcement institutions?

There's a dual answer to that question.

### 1.  Lack of Empathy and Caring

The first is the impression that many people have about police which is they simply don't care about the plight of the common person. If you're mugged, shot, had your home burglarized, the police could care less. They will come out to the scene of the crime, call out emergency services if needed, fill out the reports, and that's the extent of it. Any sort of real investigation to apprehend a suspect is few and far in-between. The survey conducted by the U.S. Department of Justice confirms that. It showed that 20% of the **violent crime** victims did not report the crime because they believed that the police "*would not or could not help.*" The lack of empathy or lack of caring by law enforcement institutions correlates then to the "**would not**" aspect of what citizens believe.

However, speaking from personal experience, that is not how it used to be. When I was a child growing up in the 1970's, our home was burglarized. Someone had broken the downstairs window, climbed through and stole some items. My parents were not rich, in fact I would characterize us as being poor, but somehow they managed to scrimp and save to put food on the table and clothes on our backs. After the police officer came out and took the report, a detective was assigned to the case.

My parents would stay in touch with him to find out the progress of the case. He visited on occasion to ask additional questions and my parents were always happy to have him over, offering cookies and coffee. With really no evidence to go on and in just a few short months, my father received a call from the detective with good news. The detective found the person who committed the crime, arrested him and he was even able to return some of our stolen items back.

That detective was a true consummate professional. He exemplified what I now know to be the Law Enforcement Code of Ethics. It states the following:

*As a Law Enforcement Officer, my fundamental duty is to serve mankind; to safeguard lives and property; to protect the innocent against deception, the weak against oppression or intimidation, and the peaceful against violence or disorder; and to respect the*

*Constitutional rights of all men to liberty, equality and justice.*

*I will keep my private life unsullied as an example to all; maintain courageous calm in the face of danger, scorn, or ridicule; develop self-restraint; and be constantly mindful of the welfare of others. Honest in thought and deed in both my personal and official life, I will be exemplary in obeying the laws of the land and the regulations of my department.*

*Whatever I see or hear of a confidential nature or that is confided to me in my official capacity will be kept ever secret unless revelation is necessary in the performance of my duty.*

*I will never act officiously or permit personal feelings, prejudices, animosities or friendships to influence my decisions. With no compromise for crime and with relentless prosecution of criminals, I will enforce the law courteously and appropriately without fear or favor, malice or ill will, never employing unnecessary force or violence and never accepting gratuities.*

*I recognize the badge of my office as a symbol of public faith, and I accept it as a public trust to be held as long as I am true to the ethics of the police service. I will constantly strive to achieve these objectives and ideals, dedicating myself before God to my chosen profession ... law enforcement.*

Let's look at the first paragraph:

*"As a Law Enforcement Officer…my fundamental duty is to serve mankind; to safeguard lives and property; to protect the innocent against deception, the weak against oppression or intimidation…"*

Do we believe that law enforcement as an institution now, tries to uphold this sacred oath in present day? That it really cares about the public, the common person, and that it tries to *"protect the innocent against deception"* or the *"weak against oppression or intimidation?"*

When the largest police union in the United States representing over 300,000 sworn officers endorses a candidate that has a history mired with thousands of lawsuits; accused by at least ten women of unwanted physical contact; when that candidate can be heard on tape talking about committing what some attorneys described as "sexual assault;" when he's urged his supporters to beat up protesters at his rallies; when he's made fun of a reporter's physical disability; when he's founded a university which one salesman called "a fraudulent scheme, and that it preyed upon the elderly and uneducated to separate them from their money;" when all those things and so much more define this person's integrity, morality, character and that individual is still endorsed by the largest police union in the United States. What does that say?

Does this candidate demonstrate the values enshrined in the Law Enforcement Code of Ethics that law enforcement officers are supposed to uphold?

How does making fun of a disabled person, for example, fit in with what the Code of Ethics says about protecting *"the weak against...intimidation?"* Or the university he operated that was described as a "fraudulent scheme...that it preyed upon the elderly...to separate them from their money" fit in with what the Code of Ethics states about *"protect[ing] the innocent against deception?"*

What can the common person take away from this law enforcement union endorsing this candidate? What message is the union and the officers it represents sending to the American public?

Is there a line in the sand where this institution and the officers it represents would not give its endorsement or would withdraw it? What if there was an allegation in which he molested children? What if he shot someone in the street? What if he killed a fellow police officer?

Where is that line for the men and women sworn to protect the ordinary citizen? Sworn to protect the weakest among us.

This was no ordinary candidate. What this person stands for, what this person encompasses is completely antithetical to the Law Enforcement Code of Ethics. Yet according to a survey conducted by Police Magazine, published September 2, 2016, 84% of working law enforcement officers stated that they would vote for this candidate in the November 2016 election.[7]

So the question becomes what does the institution stand for now? Is it the one that embodies the Code of Ethics or is it the one that embodies all that this candidate displays in his character and stands for?

Perhaps when the Code of Ethics was first written and adopted in 1957, officers believed in it, respected it and tried to uphold it. But the endorsement by this police organization sends a clear message. And to me that message is—*we are not interested in upholding the Code of Ethics, we are not interested in protecting the weak, we are not interested in protecting the innocent, we are not interested in upholding morality, we are interested in only one thing, power. Those that have it and can give it to us.*

This **endorsement** by a police union, sends a clear message by law enforcement to the public that they are abandoning the integrity, morality and decency the Code of Ethics stands for.

§

Based on everything I have shown here, the impression the public has about law enforcement not caring about the common person has a basis of truth to it.

The data outlined here would suggest that to be a valid criticism. When you have an increase in crime and millions of unsolved cases every year, coupled with the institution's views of what it deems morally and ethically acceptable and of whom it should align with, there is no other conclusion one can draw.

Let me be clear about one thing. When I use the word "law enforcement" or "institution" I am not referring to individual police officers, agents, etc. I am referring to the institutions. Of course, I understand that as individuals without the uniform on, you may not share the same view or attitude as the institution that is employing you or of the organization that is representing you. But when you put on that uniform and take orders from your commander and speak and act as one voice, so too must you be looked upon in that regard—as a group.

Whatever individuality you have, whatever beliefs you have, whatever compassion or sensitivity you may possess in your personal life, has no basis for consideration.

And the reason is very simple. If your commander orders you to break up a protest for example, even though the protesters have valid permits and are acting peacefully, would you do it? The answer is, of course, "yes." You would not challenge your commander or refuse an order. And so that is the reason. When you put on that uniform, you leave your beliefs, your ideas, in essence your "self" at home. You are now a hired professional at the disposal of your employer.

The point here is not to assign blame, but rather it's about understanding. Understanding why an institution behaves the way it does and how we can get our law enforcement institutions and our officers to care once again about the little people; to care about the poor, the middle-class, the weak, the elderly; to not see us as the enemy simply because we **ARE** poor, elderly, and weak; and to have the Code of Ethics mean something once again.

$$\int$$

## 2.   Handcuffing the Police

The second answer to this complicated question of where is our law enforcement to the common person is the notion that these institutions are being manipulated by the wealthy and powerful.

Law enforcement is being manipulated and used by the very people they should be protecting us from— the wealthy and powerful. And the surreptitious manner in which it is done is quite brilliant, so that no fault could ever be assigned. Law enforcement is not to blame however, as they are subject to the same conditions as you and me.

To get a sense of how this is being accomplished, an understanding is needed of what is presently happening in our society. Currently just the sheer force of all the evil that is present in this world is moving the line that has existed between good and bad. What was once considered bad, illegal, or morally reprehensible is now being challenged or being justified. A *"so what"* attitude is prevalent. *"What's the big deal?"* or *"How do you know for sure?"* Law enforcement is ill-equipped to deal with those types of scenarios.

What happens when law enforcement is overwhelmed, when too much bad is happening in the world, when that line is moved just by the sheer size and force of evil that exists? Human nature dictates that we accept our current predicament, that over time, it becomes the norm, that we justify it in our mind and eventually come to not see anything wrong with it. We deal with it by becoming desensitized to it. That is human nature.

§

So what happens to good when the line moves and good is under attack? Good flees. Even worse, good is like an ostrich that when faced with danger sticks its head in the sand (yes, a myth) and hopes that evil doesn't see it. That evil will choose someone else and leave it alone. Good is weak. Good is afraid. Good does not want to get involved. Good doesn't want to stand up to evil. It turns its back, hides its eyes when evil is hurting someone. Those things are not necessarily a bad thing or a criticism. That is good by definition. That is good by its nature—to turn away from evil. But good can also be strong. Good can and does encompass the weak, the strong and everything in-between.

Now, as the line shifts, bad people perceive that law enforcement is either lacking the resources or the will to deal with the shift, so they do bad. As they get away with doing the bad, overtime, that act is no longer perceived as something out of the norm. As that gets digested by society and accepted, the line begins to move. Police become more overwhelmed so they move with the line to the new norm as well. Bad people see where the new line is and they begin to test its limits, to see whether there will be a reaction by law enforcement or if they are too busy, too inundated to react. If too overwhelmed, the line gets moved again. And the cycle continues.

So now instead of the police being the guardians of law, of justice and of the morality set by society in which we live, they are now just watchers themselves.

They see the line moving just as we all see it in society and whether we like it or not, we just accept it. So where is this line now you might ask? What is considered right and wrong? What act/event will law enforcement come to the rescue of? I couldn't answer that right now as that line is moving to the side of evil very fast. But take comfort in that murder is still frowned upon and law enforcement will answer the call for that (see endnote).[8]

Law enforcement just doesn't have the necessary resources to **investigate and obtain the evidence** that someone stole your purse, committed fraud, and burglarized your home. Fifty years ago, if any of those things occurred, you can rest assured that you had the full attention of the police, your neighbors, and society. Now, it would be laughable to even bother calling the police about such matters in some areas of the country, let alone someone actually solving that crime.

§

While law enforcement will still answer the call for murder, whether law enforcement will put resources into something else depends on so many things. It's no longer about what the crime is. It also depends on who you are (rich/poor, famous/unknown), the powers that be in that particular area, politics, media exposure, how much of a political threat you are to the powers that be, etc. All of this plays a role in whether law enforcement **chooses** to defend that line **for you** or not. But don't blame law enforcement; they are doing their best with the resources they have and the control they are under.

## Who Owns the Law?

So just who is law enforcement beholden to? The wealthy and powerful of course. The wealthy and powerful have taken over and crippled the institution. How did they do that?

Well, if I make $50,000 per year and one percent of the tax goes to law enforcement, then that would be $500. Now suppose I make $20,000,000 per year, then my tax contribution to law enforcement is $200,000. Who is going to have more control over law enforcement? I can guess what you're thinking—that it's ludicrous to believe that anyone would have any control over law enforcement, especially given that this money is taxes so it's paid anonymously. Agreed.

However, the scenario doesn't stop there. This wealthy taxpayer also happens to join a group: a group whose purpose is to reduce taxes on himself. He makes contributions to this group and so do a lot of wealthy taxpayers. They also get one of their wealthy friends or anyone that looks and speaks the part and aligns with their agenda to run for government office. And thanks to those generous campaign contributions and Super PACs[9], a lot of these candidates make it into office.

These newly elected individuals are now your government. They have control and/or influence over what happens to the tax money the government collects. They control the money, which means they have the power. So now, they get to decide one of two things when it comes to these wealthy individual's tax burden. They could say to these wealthy individuals that their overall tax burden is too great, so instead of the 30% that they are paying with 1% of it going towards law enforcement, they now only have to pay 20%, which means of course that we can't have 1% continue to go towards law enforcement, so we'll have to cut that to .5%. Or if these powerful individuals that now control government or at least have influence aren't successful with getting overall taxes for the rich reduced, they could reallocate the funds. So instead of 1% going towards law enforcement, it's now .5%.

And the reasons cited would run the gamut such as: *"the military needs the money to fund a war, the economy is slowing, not enough taxes are coming in, etc."*

With the institution now in the hands of the wealthy and powerful, (although still appearing to be in the hands of citizens), law enforcement budgets get decimated and are unable to keep up with what is needed to keep the societal good/bad line from moving. Law enforcement then must prioritize.

§

While the politician's primary goal is to lessen the tax burden on the wealthy, a by-product and a benefit to the wealthy is now law enforcement must use their limited resources to handle violent crimes first, while non-violent crimes become secondary. This clears the path for white-collar crimes such as fraud of the common person and other questionable financial offenses.

Can you think of a more plausible reason why government, the instrument that controls law enforcement, allows the good/bad line to move in its society? We talked about crime that has elements of violence in it and that this thankfully is still enforced by the police and gets media attention. What is not talked about and rarely investigated are the non-violent crimes, the white-collar crimes if you will, that are perpetrated by individuals and companies that will never see the light of day in a court room. They are too hard to investigate, too hard to prove.

Non-violent crimes perpetrated by the privileged, the wealthy, are usually against the poor, the middle-class, the elderly, and the uninformed. There's not enough resources, and not enough money available by law enforcement to investigate. The common person is left defenseless, forced to pursue justice in civil court; an avenue that usually requires money. Something the common person doesn't have.

It is open season on anyone and everyone who is decent, weak (not a bad word), powerless, or helpless;

open season on that good/bad line. Why do the wealthy and powerful do this? Greed of course:

*"I'm not happy with the money I'm making, so I'll take yours too. I don't care if I hurt you. I don't care if you eat cat food. It's your tough luck."*

This arrangement is brilliantly disguised under the umbrella of a million different reasons. Reasons such as *"The government is on the verge of bankruptcy. Bad guys are adapting. Bad guys are sophisticated. Everyone is hurting."* You name it, every excuse has been used. But informed individuals understand that these are all smoke screens. The wealthy and powerful have crippled the institution that was designed to provide fairness and justice, to defend the poor and innocent, to protect good people from evil. After all, what other mechanisms in our society exists to contain man's moral compass when men cannot or will not do it themselves? But when law enforcement is weakened, there is nothing left to stop evil from flourishing. Edmund Burke said, "The only thing necessary for the triumph of evil is for good men to do nothing."

§

The wealthy have no interest in helping protect the poor, the elderly, and the weak from crime. Their sole purpose in utilizing these strategies is very simple: to make money and keep money. Beyond that, they could care less about the impact they are having on society, or about the plight of their fellow citizens.

They've checked out of being a part of the human race. They would sooner live in isolated bubbles away from everyone if they could. Let everyone else fight for whatever scraps are left. So the poor stealing from the poor, the middle-class stealing from the poor, and the rich stealing from middle-class, anything goes and law enforcement is too busy dealing with real matters.

But let anyone do harm to a wealthy and powerful individual and you can guarantee that law enforcement resources will come to bear. Whether we like it or not, this is our reality.

§

For those wealthy individuals who might be insulted by this, I ask you: if your safety was on the line or even your financial health and the government came to you and said that they'll need to raise your taxes by billions of dollars in order to hire more police to protect **you**, would you pay it? You'd say "yes" in a heartbeat. So why aren't you doing it now? The answer is because it's not advantageous for you. Quite the opposite, more benefit is derived from a weak judicial system; one that is controlled by you, where you can direct where resources should go and can explain it to the public—*that the police have a shoestring budget, and violent crime will have to be the priority and everything else must take a back seat.*

That is how the wealthy and powerful have taken control of government, and hijacked law enforcement. And how they are responsible for the lack of resources that law enforcement needs to keep up with crime and protect even the poorest, weakest among us in an effort to prevent evil from taking root.

§

The police officer on the street or the agent in the field deserves our utmost respect and gratitude.

§

Individuals working in law enforcement are people just like you and me. They have families, a spouse, children, and parents. They risk their lives every day in an effort to keep evil at bay. Without them, good would have been stamped out of society a long time ago.

§

# Chapter 7
# The Transfer of Matter

What's happening with wealth transfer can be compared to what happens in a binary star system. In a binary star system, two stars are orbiting a center point. As the two stars come within proximity of each other, the bigger star having a stronger gravitational pull will cause the transfer of matter from the smaller star to the bigger one. This matter will be absorbed into the bigger one. As the bigger star grows even bigger and the smaller star gets even smaller, the gravitational pull of the bigger star gets even stronger so that each time the stars get within proximity of each other, even more and more matter gets pulled.

Eventually, the smaller star will give up all its matter to the bigger one and thus will cease to exist.

This is what is happening with wealth.

❧

So, let's put this in context of data we can understand. The bottom half of the world's population—**3.5 billion people**—own the same as the richest **85 people** in the world.[10]

In 2010, the bottom 90% of the world's population owned 17% of the world's wealth.[11] In 2016 the bottom 90% of the world's population now own just 11% of the world's wealth.[12]

The bottom 50% of adults collectively own less than 1% of the world's wealth.[13]

The top **one** percent now own over **50%** of the world's wealth.[14]

**In the U.S., the wealthiest one percent captured 95 percent of post-financial crisis growth since 2009, while the bottom 90 percent became poorer.** [15]

In the United States in 2012:

160,000 families own 22% of the total wealth in this country.[16]

The top **one** percent own **42%** of the total wealth in the country.[17]

The top **ten** percent own **77%** of the total wealth in the country.[18]

What about the remaining **90%** of the population in the United States? Well they own just **23%**.[19]

**One tenth of one percent or 160,700 families in the United States own more than 145,000,000 American families combined.**[20]

§

In 1969 the top **one** percent owned 34.4% of the wealth in the U.S. In 2007, the top one percent owned 34.6% of the wealth; virtually unchanged in 38 years.[21]

But from 2007 to 2012 that figure has gone up to **41.8%**.[22] And while there is no current data available yet for 2016 on the United States, it is highly likely that in the last four years we have witnessed a greater acceleration of wealth inequality in the United States.

My guess would be that today, the top one percent now own 50% of the wealth in the United States in keeping with the world figure.

Astounding to think that in just nine short years, the top one percent in the United States could have managed to capture an additional 15% of the total wealth. That would truly be an unbelievable feat of enormous proportions.

§

If you view total wealth as a pie and everyone sharing in that pie, then what you have is one percent of the population taking half of the pie leaving the remaining half of the pie to be shared by 99% of the population.

Every time the wealthy increase their share, they are essentially taking a bigger slice of the pie, which leaves less and less for the rest of us to share.

So, there's no question that there has been a transfer of money but what's astonishing is the rate of acceleration. What can this be attributed to? Why are the rich getting richer and the poor getting poorer?

§

But an even more important question, how many millions or billions of dollars does one person need? Too often, what you find in our society is the middle-class helping the poor. The rich all have their charitable organizations or foundations if you will that they form and be a part of to make themselves feel good and to look good. And then they delve it in dribs and drabs. Yes, I know I'm going to get comments that say something like *"We gave millions of dollars last year, is that dribs and drabs?"* Well in the context of how much the top one percent earns and owns, the answer would be yes, it's dribs and drabs.

This isn't about going after the wealthy, it's about asking the question, *how much is too much*? And where is this need to hoard money coming from? You can have too much coffee, too much ice cream, but never too much money? What value is being derived from having all this money sitting in a bank account or in some other asset somewhere? Money that you can't take with you when you die and that you have no hope of ever spending in your lifetime: hundreds of millions of dollars, even billions of dollars just sitting in bank accounts. And no matter how much you try to spend it, the interest alone from that money is more than you can actually spend.

So why do they do this? The reason the wealthy keep such vast amounts of money with no real hope of spending it is because money translates into power. It's like the government having a massive number of nuclear missiles; enough missiles to destroy the world ten times over and with no real plan to ever use them. That's what money is to the wealthy. It's the nuclear option for them. It is both an offensive weapon (in case you want to go after someone or something; even an idea) and a defensive weapon to prevent your enemies from coming after you.

§

Meanwhile, there are starving people, homeless people, people who are suffering from indignities, people who are living paycheck to paycheck, and compassion for them seems to be waning with each passing day while at the same time our intolerance and disdain for them is growing.

So, I'd like to say to the wealthy: Do you realize that during your life, you've let millions upon millions of people go homeless or starve when you could have helped—if only you hadn't argued with and controlled the government and allowed it to tax you appropriately or inappropriately if that's what you believe? Instead, you've joined a party and made contributions to that party whose goal was to influence the government and get it to stop taxing you so much or to put candidates into office who also share your viewpoint.

Would it be so bad if after taxes, your income for the year was $15 million instead of $17 million? Of course not. Would it have affected your life dramatically or even at all? Not a bit. But greed has taken a hold of your soul and reduced you to a mere shell of a person. Ask yourself if your existence at this time and in this place helped or hurt your fellow man?

The fact that from 1969 to 2007 the top one percent owned relatively the same amount of wealth (plus or minus a few percentage points) suggests something that is **unquantifiable** but true.

And that is where the **wealthy in the past** (old money) used to feel a sense of obligation to society; where there used to exist an understood contract between them and the middle-class; where the wealthy felt a sense of moral obligation; where the wealthy managed to curtail their greed guided by integrity and a sense of right and wrong; where the wealthy were more likely to share some of their wealth with the working middle-class; where all those things used to exist have now been replaced by a **new generation of wealthy** that believe that greed is good; that whatever implicit contract existed in the past between them and the middle-class is now **null and void**; that believe if I can make it why can't you; that it's all about "self-responsibility;" that I have no moral obligation to the society in which I live; that our financial system demands that I be ruthless in my economic pursuits; that I must do whatever it takes for the almighty dollar irrespective of the harm that it may have upon others living in the same country, in the same city, in the same suburb, even on the same street.

§

Saez and Zucman state that "Despite population aging, the rich are younger today than half a century ago," noting that the "...rapid increase in wealth at the top is the surge in the share of income, in particular labor income, earned by top wealth holders."[23]

To me this confirms my earlier assertion that this new breed of wealthy individuals are guided by a different set of values from their previous predecessors: That as a group, they give no thought or consideration to anyone other than themselves.

There is a real uncomfortableness when you ask the wealthy to talk about money and try and connect it to the suffering of other people. The wealthy would love to compartmentalize the two as if there is absolutely no connection between their greed and human suffering. As if somehow their money came from a tree somewhere and not from other people. And so by compartmentalizing the two, by saying that there is no connection between the two, between their greed and the poverty of others, they are in essence elevating money over human beings.

§

In fact, this new breed of wealthy feel they have a duty to pay as little taxes as possible, even avoid it if they can. They would prefer to hire companies and lobbyists and spend millions of dollars all in pursuit of minimizing their tax burden. And if social programs like food stamps have to be cut, who cares.

You hear of companies that move their headquarters overseas to another country (aka corporate inversion) all so they can avoid paying taxes. For those companies that are now controlled by this new breed that feel as I have just described, it's all about extraction. Extracting money from society and never putting anything in. If everyone did that, just took money out and never put money back in, what would our world look like? What would your town look like?

§

The mindset that we have is that greed is good, that everyone needs to behave as greedy and opportunistic in order for our capitalist system to function properly. Any other type of thought is labeled "socialism." However, that is a myth! What you were taught from a very early age is simply wrong—greed is not good. In order for capitalism to work, there must be balance in the system. Capitalism requires that there be social contracts among those with power and those without (This is explained later in the book).

§

We have placed a higher value on money than on human beings. A piece of paper is now so important that I don't care if you starve. In the world we live in today, it's "every man, every woman, every child for himself/herself!"

And in this game called life (it's not a game but to the wealthy it is), the deck has been stacked against the majority. Yes, there are cases when one person becomes rich, but that's like winning the lottery.

When such a thing happens, you can rest assured that the wealthy and media are the first to publicize such stories to keep everyone in line and give hope, "*See this person did it, so can you.*" Pointing out rare cases of success portrays them as somehow attainable, but more than that it makes it seem common, as though anyone can do it and that a lot of people do achieve it. In reality though, it's a false hope. You wouldn't advise someone to spend his or her money on lottery tickets every day, would you?

Knowing that there is a 99.9% chance that they will lose their money every day they play, would you tout those statistics as being great? No, of course not.

While there is a chance that a person can become successful, statistically speaking, 99% are not going to be successful. The fact is, the vast majority of hard working people are not going to become wealthy. So let's not continue to dangle a successful person to the average hard-working person like we dangle a carrot in front of a horse, because the reality is, statistics do not support it.

§

Almost every religion that exists states in one form or another that we must all help our fellow man. Yet in this country, there are people who say that we are all responsible for ourselves. That if we are poor, homeless, out of work, hungry, we are to blame. "Lazy" is the most common term, along with "Get a job." Never mind that there are 10 million people looking for a job, but only one million jobs available. Let's just ignore that fact. It's easier to just blame "them" and say that there must be something wrong with "them;" that they need to take responsibility for themselves. That government should not help. These groups of callous individuals are unable to reconcile their religious beliefs with their political ideology. As a result, they do not want to be questioned. They do not want a spotlight shined on them because they are the epitome of hypocrisy.

§

With the wealthy in power and in control of government, this gives rise and clears the path for a transfer of money from the middle-class to the rich—a squeezing of the poor and middle-class. If anyone dares to speak up about it, the wealthy have lots of followers they can send out with a list of statements, like *"Everyone is on welfare and I don't want my taxes going towards social programs. Everyone should be able to get a job. Immigrants are coming over and stealing our jobs. Etc."*

Meanwhile, the rich are laughing all the way to the bank as they get these uninformed people to do all their dirty work for them. The sad part about this is that these hard working, tax paying individuals have no idea that they are being used, being manipulated by the wealthy and powerful. These individuals believe on some level that they are on equal footing with the wealthy and powerful. If they actually paid attention to policies, to facts, they would see that their support of these rich and powerful individuals would be a real, quantifiable financial hurt to themselves and their families. Evil is a very powerful force employing any number of tactics, such as trickery, and is masterful at feeding your ego to achieve its objectives.

§

# Chapter 8
# The Existence of Life After Death

In the constant battle of good versus evil, evil will always win. Do you know why? Because there is nothing evil won't do, no limitations, no lines that it won't cross to succeed. Good, however, has a line. There are things that good cannot do, a line that it won't cross, for if it did, it would cease to be good.

§

That is the age-old dilemma. How does good fight evil without itself becoming evil? If I truly come face to face with the Devil himself and I have a chance to slay him, to end his existence once and for all and thus save humanity, how can I? How can I find the justification to do that? If I do, then what am I? Am I still good? Have I crossed that line? Without a doubt, the answer is yes. I cease to be good. Never cause harm to anyone! Why?

First, our thoughts and knowledge about our existence and the universe is minuscule. Assuming that you have sufficient knowledge to make a decision like causing harm to another individual is without a doubt, flawed.

Second, we have very little understanding of what lies ahead after this life. You are presupposing that your sole existence is rooted only in this moment and on this planet. What if your existence now is merely a passageway to something greater that you will get to experience after this life? There is so much anecdotal evidence that something else exists in the afterlife that cannot be ignored. You or someone you know has probably experienced something that is unexplainable. I have certainly and am happy to share this personal story with you.

I had been dating a woman for many years and became close with her parents, especially her father. He was a kindhearted man, full of life, and always cheerful. He was a carpenter by trade and loved working with his hands, as did I. Many times, we would work on projects together for our homes. He was an old school Italian who would often say the phrase "Forget about it." I thought it quite amusing. For example, if I said, "Thank you for helping me move this flagstone." He would reply "Forget about it." It was his way of saying "You're welcome."

But sadly, one day in his 70's, he died. No more would he be around to help with projects. Shortly after his death, I had a dream about him. In the dream he kept saying, "Forget about it" but he would say it in all sorts of varying ways. Like "For gett aabout it," "Fooor gettta about it" as if it was being said in slow motion. That was the whole dream, just him saying that to me. Now you might think, what's so special about that? It was just a dream because you just lost someone you cared about. And yes, I would agree with you except something else happened outside of this dream at that exact moment I was having this dream.

You see, the day before I had this dream, we went to the grocery store and got some apples that we placed on the kitchen counter. This was not unusual. The apples were sitting on the counter for the better part of at least 12 hours prior to my dream: Just sitting there, undisturbed on the counter **in the back** near the wall. Now what is truly remarkable is that at the exact moment that I was having this dream, an apple, all by itself, rolls off the counter and hits the floor waking me up—which is the reason why I remember this dream so vividly. I get up right away to investigate the noise and to my surprise it was an apple on the floor.

Had it not been for the apple rolling off the counter all by itself, hitting the floor and waking me up, there is a very good chance that I may not have remembered the dream. Because as you know, sometimes we have dreams and when we wake up, we can't remember them.

§

So, is it a coincidence that an apple that had been sitting there for the better part of 12 hours, magically starts to roll off the counter on its own, hitting the floor and waking me up at the exact moment I'm having this dream? Perhaps, but my god what a fantastic coincidence that is! What gives credence and makes this story so powerful is the way these two events that have no causal relationship with each other (that is the dream didn't cause the apple to fall nor did the apple falling contribute to my having a dream) intersect with each other at such a moment in time as to be completely impactful. I interpreted what took place as his way of letting me know that everything is all right, that I don't need to worry.

If I interpret what took place as being his actions; that I wasn't having a "dream" but rather it was him giving me a message and making sure that I would remember it by dropping that apple on the floor, then one must conclude that there must be an existence or life beyond this one.

§

This is my own personal story but I can bet that all of you have had some experience of unexplained phenomenon or know someone that has. There are numerous accounts written by so many different people.

Whether we want to see it or not, our existence on this planet is a mere blip and of no real consequential value. Look at the vastness of all we can comprehend. The universe is 13.7 **billion** years old. Earth is 4.5

**billion** years old. From the beginning of man as Homo sapiens some 50,000 B.C. to now, it is estimated that about 75-100 billion people have lived and died here. And in this endless space of time, we live and we will die just like everyone else now buried in cemeteries throughout the world. You and I exist for a mere 100 years and in a few hundred years after we're gone, no one will remember us.

What do you want your life to be about? Do you want your life to be full of anger, hatred, and venom?

Supposing for a minute that there is life after death, do you ever think about that specific group of people that will be there? Which group? The wealthy bad people; the ones with all the money and power; the ones that made others suffer; the ones that looked down on people, pretended to care when in reality did not give a darn; the ones who could have shared their fortunes and thus improve the lives of so many people around them, but instead chose the path of greed and gluttony; the ones that usher in hell on earth whether by intention or ignorance. And if by ignorance then it's a refusal to think whether in fact their actions are hurting others or not; purposefully trying to avoid seeing what the outcome of their actions looks like. No need to look someone in the face as you take their money; or squeeze them so much that they live a life of merely just existing, all for your own benefit.

§

Imagine those wealthy, unscrupulous individuals in the afterlife, without their money or power. Where do you suppose their arrogance is, their smugness, and their righteousness? In the afterlife, they are now truly equal to a homeless man. They are nothing special, certainly no more special than anyone else.

Make your life a positive one. One full of compassion and understanding for your fellow man—in whatever small way you can.

If you believe that there is "**life**" after death, that your existence just doesn't end when you die, then what you are also saying is that you have a **soul**. A **soul**!

§

# Chapter 9
# Understanding Our World and What is Possible

*Love. Think about that feeling for a minute.*

*Hate. Think about that feeling for a minute.*

*What's in your heart for your fellow man?*

Competition over things, mostly money, brings out feelings of hate towards our fellow man. This immense need to survive to the exclusion of **everything** else is why hate exists. And with hate, comes justification.

The two go hand in hand. First, I must paint you so that you do not appear to be like me. Then I can justify any action I want to take towards you.

Now imagine a world where competition no longer exists; where my getting something does not take away from you getting something, even the same thing.

While you may not see this, the wealthy have turned us into play toys. We are there to amuse them, dance for them, jump as high as they want us to, and do all their dirty work for them. Want monumental proof? Let's look at the Gulf Wars.

§

## Puppets of the Wealthy

In August 1990, Iraq invaded Kuwait. What do we know about Kuwait? Kuwait has the sixth largest oil reserves in the world. It has a population of 3.9 million of which 1.3 million are Kuwaiti **citizens**. The rest are considered "expatriates." It has one of the highest per capita income with the Kuwait Dinar (their currency) being the highest valued currency in the world (1 Dinar =$3.30 USD). The country and its citizens are so rich that for the most part, they don't work. Its government is a monarchy headed by one ruling family with one man, the Emir as the head ruler.

So what do they do when it comes to manual labor such as building roads, hotels, housekeeping, etc.? They actually bring in people from other countries such as India and Pakistan to do their work for them. In fact, nearly 70% of the population or 2.6 million people living there are "expatriates" — people brought in from other countries to service the 1.3 million Kuwaiti citizens.

When Iraq invaded Kuwait, Kuwait did what Kuwait does and hired the United States along with a few other countries to fight its war. The wealthy and powerful that control the U.S. Government came to the aid of this wealthy country. It was decided that the United States would risk the lives of its citizens, essentially becoming a hired gun for the wealthy Kuwaiti.

While this was happening, the Kuwaitis essentially just sat there and let the United States fight their war for them. In exchange for us fighting their war, they paid $32 billion. Ask yourself, if Kuwait weren't a rich country able to pay, if they had no oil reserves, would the United States have fought their war?

§

What about the second Gulf War, when the entire country was deceived into thinking Saddam Hussein had nuclear weapons? Who benefited from that war? Well, I can think of a few companies that produce weapons and provide other services during war time (collectively known as the "military-industrial complex"). Essentially, it was the wealthy and powerful once again, who greatly benefited from the mayhem and destruction.

What about our soldiers who risked their lives? Did they share in those profits? No, of course not. Hundreds of billions of dollars paid to those companies—money that came from taxpayers and *transferred* to the wealthy and powerful.

Think about the hundreds of millions of people that work every day for someone else that will never share in profits.

## The Story of Greed

This is a constant theme in our history: the wealthy and powerful getting even wealthier and even more powerful off the backs of ordinary people. The destruction of our civilization is occurring right before our very eyes by the wealthy, but because they have included us, because we also share in their pie (albeit a very small sliver and getting smaller every year thanks to greed), because our survival and that of our children are dependent on them, we cannot find the strength, nor the will to challenge them. Essentially, we are on crack and they are the crack dealers.

§

Every once in a while, we think we can go cold turkey, we think we can stand up to them by demanding higher wages or better benefits or asking for better working conditions. But they get mad, their ego and their greed kicks right in and they show us just who's boss by punishing us, by closing factories and shipping jobs overseas.

I imagine them thinking:

*"That will teach you to speak up to me. You should have just accepted the miserable wages and miserable benefits we were giving you. Now you have nothing. How dare you speak to me that way? You take whatever sliver of pie I decide to give you. I don't care if it's not enough to feed your family. And I will tell you what to think and how to think. And if I tell you to believe that immigrants are stealing your jobs, then by God that's what you better believe. And believe it down to your core: Or else. Got it?"*

This is what the American worker particularly in the Midwest and the South has had to endure—a brainwashing in effect by the wealthy upon the working class. A constant bombardment of propaganda, fiction, and non-truths through the media, so frequent and so often that you start to believe it. It takes a toll upon your psyche, upon your ability to tell fact from fiction.

§

Some people look back at WWII and say, "How could a whole country be brainwashed to go along with a mad man like Hitler?" They think that if we had lived during that time and in that place, we would have behaved differently. But the mere promise of prosperity when you are starving is all that is needed for a society to willingly give up its morality and blindly believe anything without question, no matter what mad man has taken the stage. Any hope is better than no hope.

§

When there is talk about jobs leaving the country, being outsourced, cheap labor overseas, automation or immigrants stealing jobs from hard working Americans, we never flip that coin over and see just what's on the other side. We let the magicians (better known as politicians, companies, and the media) perform their voodoo magic of deception upon us. And what are they trying to convince us of?

Well here is a snippet of the potpourri of reasons we are given: *your fellow poor immigrant neighbor is to blame, he's stealing your job*. If a democrat is in the White House, then *the democrats are to blame*; the opposite is true if it's a republican. If it's a company speaking, it will tell you that *it needs to be competitive in this global environment so it needs to go where there is cheap labor.* And we believe it all.

But what's the real truth? What's on the other side of that coin that they don't want us to see? It's very simple: wealth. The privileged few are never satisfied making what they've made last year. **There must be growth!!!** Their bonuses, salaries, and the company's profits need to be better than last year. With profit being the dominant and overwhelming force of most companies, you then become an **irrelevant object**.

§

In our current economic system, we are taught from a very early age that greed is good. Movies have been made that teach us that greed is good; that we should embrace this very notion even when ten percent of the population owns 90% of the wealth. We are taught that this is normal; this is good.

But in order for greed to flourish, it can't appear too obvious. So, if a pharmaceutical company ups its price of a lifesaving drug by 5000%, well that's too obvious. The company didn't follow the proper protocol of disguising its greed. There is a method, a strategy, which involves politicians, lobbyists, and the media. When the wool is about to be pulled over your eyes, the magician needs his assistant, his dancers, lighting, and so on to distract you. The same goes here.

A story is told in which greed is cleverly disguised as something else. Something like *the company will go under if it doesn't ship jobs overseas*. Or how about the one told by politicians that immigrants are coming over and stealing your jobs. When I hear politicians say this, I never hear the journalist asking the most basic question: how is the immigrant **stealing** the job? Is he doing it with a gun like a bank robber or is it done in the middle of the night when no one is looking?

It seems to me that it's impossible to steal a job. You actually have to be hired to get a job. So who is hiring that immigrant? Is it a company, a business owner? Who is really responsible for you losing your job to an immigrant? Is it the immigrant or the person who hired him? That point is always lost in the media.

§

We are more comfortable blaming the immigrant than the actual culprit: the greedy company, or the greedy business owner who hired someone else at cheaper wages. We don't fault the wealthy owner because we have been raised to see greed as good, as necessary in our economic society; that if we were that business owner, we would do the same thing.

What we are upset about is that the wealthy business owner had a choice in the first place between a hard-working American and an immigrant. *"Darn that government for letting that immigrant into the country so that the wealthy owner had an opportunity to hire someone else at cheap labor. If they only didn't do that, I would have my job now."*

§

## The Magic of Politics

What you are not seeing in this very complicated cogwheel is the other cog, the other tooth of that gear. Just who runs the government? Just whose interest does the government official really represent? Who contributed to that politician's campaign? Who poured tons of money into getting that politician elected in the first place? Who keeps that politician well-funded so long as that politician does what they want him to do, which is to allow immigrants into the country so that they can drive down wages? Who benefited from the politician voting the way that he did?

Certainly not you! You guessed it, the wealthy, the business owner, and the company. So you see, those immigrants being allowed to come into the country and compete for your job wasn't just an accident or coincidence; it was deliberately designed to benefit one group and one group only—the wealthy and powerful. It puts more money in their bank account and leaves you without a job.

§

To the uninformed eye, it looked like there was no connection between the group that benefited from the low labor and the politicians who were given instructions (a mandate) by that group to increase immigration. And all along, you thought that the politician represented you and that he was looking out for your best interest.

But those politicians don't see it that way. To them, they see it as if they were hired/employed by that wealthy group to do what they want and that they have absolutely no obligation to you to do anything to help you. Their accountability is only to the wealthy that financed their campaign to get them elected.

§

Sure, in order to get elected, they had to tell you a whole bunch of lies and make false promises in order to make you feel like they'll represent you, but that's just politics. Once they are elected, all that goes right out the window.

That is the genius of the wealthy and powerful and our politicians. They've become masterful magicians at performing sleight of hand tricks, getting you to focus over here on one thing, while they're doing something else over there. They are so good at being magicians, that even if someone pointed out their trick, you would still find it hard to believe that it was all an illusion.

## Turning Fear into Hate

Beyond this, politicians and the wealthy have also tapped into our inner most awful selves; they have gotten us to turn on each other. They prey upon the weak, the fearful, and the uninformed. They understand humans better than we understand ourselves.

They understand that underneath our individual identities, we are basically made up of the same things. We don't just possess positive traits. No, our makeup as humans consists of having an ego, of having fear, of being able to hate, and of being able to see ourselves as superior to others.

So as a species, we can easily be persuaded to turn on each other by tapping into our negative traits. Our anger, our fears, our hatred is turned onto our neighbors; onto people that don't look like us, act like us, or worship like us; onto people just like you and me; people who have **no power**; people facing the same hardships; people who have nothing you can take from them. But because a group with power tells you that those are your enemies, you believe them.

Isn't it conceivable that a group of intelligent, wealthy individuals who knows these things can manipulate a percentage of our society and bring out these evil notions? Of course it is. In fact, they are masters at it. And with some of us having such huge egos and an aversion to self-reflection, it makes it quite easy for them.

Just 0.7% of the population owns 45.2% of the world's wealth. As a result, we let a privileged few control the majority. The majority of which are continually stressed, continually fighting for scraps, continually trying to strive for something better.

An elaborate infrastructure has been built in which government and law enforcement are there to protect them first and foremost (sure, law enforcement and government also helps the common person to a degree. Can you imagine the appearances if it didn't)? And we just accept it. "That's the way it is."

§

## Enough for Everyone

We are brainwashed. From birth, we are indoctrinated to believe that there must be competition with our fellow humans in order to survive, to get ahead in the world, to make something of yourself; to have money so you can buy a nice car and a nice house. But what makes it this way? Why does it have to be this way? There's enough food to feed the entire planet, enough land and resources to build a home for every single family. There's more than enough of everything, so we don't need to compete with one another to live happily. We can live a stress-free life (not a work free life), where our families, our children, and our souls are the main focus.

§

Some people say that if we follow this approach, we will become stagnant in our technology, in our ingenuity. Perhaps this would be true to some degree, but so what? To what end are we seeking all this technology? To what end are we seeking all this knowledge? How is working 60 hours a week to develop a newer version of a tablet or a smartphone helping mankind?

Why not enrich our souls instead of our bank accounts? Why not start laughing and playing with your children? Or truly looking into your partner's eyes and making love to them so your souls intertwine into something magical!

Think about it. Your time on this planet is finite. How are you helping humanity by unraveling the mysteries of the world? The more important question is—at what cost? What will it cost you to work 45 years non-stop until you retire?

And on this life's path that you've embarked upon, that you were programmed to undertake and expected to by society, you left this world with 2.5 children to carry on your genes. *But what purpose was it for*? What makes your genes so special that they need to be continued? What benefit have you derived from knowing that your genes will somehow continue? What was it all for? All that work, all those sacrifices.

Instead of making your life about the now, you've made your life about the future. What do you believe the top 1 percent (the wealthy) are doing while you're at work? Do you think they too are wasting their life in an office somewhere working? Maybe, but they've also gotten to see and enjoy so much more than you'll ever get to in your lifetime.

Their life is lived in the present while your life is lived under obligation and stress. After all, you've created new life even though at the time you didn't have two nickels to rub together, but you had the expectation that you would earn enough to support them for at least 18 years. You've intentionally tied an albatross around your neck. The sad part is, the part you don't realize is that you've actually helped the wealthy stay wealthy. Since profit is derived from consumption, your children are more mouths to feed, more people to clothe, buy gadgets for, etc. And when they become adults, they too will spend and consume. And who do you think benefits from all of this? Yes, the top 1%. Every purchase you make, every penny you spend, some percentage of that money makes its way back to them.

§

So, without fully realizing it at the time, you have voluntarily placed yourself in a life of servitude and enriched the pockets of the wealthy—not only by what you will spend to take care of your children, but by what they will spend as adults.

Yes, I understand the need for family, how enriching it is to have children and to love, but this book is about seeing things from a practical perspective. And since there are books that solely speak about the importance of family life, it is only fair that I get to talk just about the practical side.

It's time to give some thought to the implications of your actions beyond just your immediate family. We don't live in bubbles where our choices have no effect on anyone or anything else. As everyone lives with the same sense of a family unit being autonomous and having no impact on anyone or anything else, what we end up with is problems—problems that have a greater impact. Billions of "autonomous" families, but all inhabiting one planet, all consuming the same food sources, all trying to occupy the same space, all breathing the same air and no one daring to look outside of their bubble. And all of those people saying, "Let the other person do something about it— it's not my problem."

Our planet is small, and getting smaller with each new birth.

§

Beyond having a nice home and food on the table and decent clothes, there is no value derived from anything else. We have been programmed to consume things. Things that in the end, you can't take with you in the afterlife. Things that become outdated in a year's time, yet the moment it comes out, you have to have it. Things that keep you preoccupied so time can pass by without you realizing it. Things that interfere with you having a deep connection with your children, your spouse, and your friends.

§

We are headed down a horrible road. Our extinction will come, but not in the form of a bomb or other catastrophic event. It will come through evolution.

The combination of our intelligence, hatred, anger, greed and ego forms a potent mixture. So potent in fact, that we can quite literally evolve to cause our own extinction.

For example, if we were to go extinct because of nuclear war or some other catastrophic event of our own doing, most people would probably attribute that as the reason—nuclear war or whatever that event was. While that may be the reason on the surface, the actual origin would be the combination of all our traits, of what we evolved into and became: that we were intelligent enough to create such a bomb capable of annihilation, combined with our hatred for one another along with greed for power or money along with ego that most of us are unable to control and in many respects, claims our soul as its own.

So in essence, the real cause would be that we evolved to a point as to cause our own demise.

Or will we evolve, not go extinct, but become so aggressive and hateful with each other that we end up rooting out our very own souls? That we basically end up as nothing more than animals.

And while our history is full of atrocities, those are nothing compared to what we can become. What I'm fighting for here is for us to recognize that we have souls we must protect and nurture. Why are our souls forgotten in favor of survival? Why is it a choice? Why not both? We remember our souls on our deathbed when it's time to go. When we ask people and God to forgive us for all we have done.

§

Most of us see ourselves as nice, kind, compassionate, loving people. So how is it that as individuals, we see ourselves this way, but as a race, based on our history, we're truly atrocious creatures committing genocide, mass murders, killings, torture, and letting children starve? How can there be such a disconnect between the two? Somewhere, someone is not being honest with themselves.

§

Logically speaking, do you see the path that we're on as sustainable, as smart, as the only road that we were meant to be on as a species?

It would not be right of me to tell you how dire our world is without offering a solution. This solution is about more than saving our planet—it's about saving our souls; but not by using religion, rather by practical, logical means. It's about saving humanity and it's about evolution. Evolving to a higher plane than what we once were. We don't need to be remembered (not sure by whom) as the atrocious, despicable creatures that once inhabited this planet.

§

# Chapter 10
# Ending the Use of Money

## Solution One

Throughout time, it's always been the few controlling the masses. But how can a few have such control?

The answer is because the few have money. And money translates into so many things. With money, you can have an army, weapons, food, and propaganda. You can teach children what you want, you can indoctrinate your philosophy, your way of thinking, and your beliefs.

In our society, everyone works for money. It's conceivable then to have the reverse (not the inverse). Everyone works for no money. What's the difference?

There is no difference, except that with the money scenario, you've built in a competition mechanism.

What would happen if we eliminated money altogether? If the concept itself no longer existed. Imagine a world with no bills, no pressures, where anytime you wanted food, you simply went down to your local grocery store, picked up what you needed and walked out. Where you stop at a gas station, fill up your car; no need to pay, just drive away.

In this new world, the term "money" is a foreign concept.

§

The farmer harvests his crops and gives it away to the distributor, who in turn gives it away to various grocery stores, including the grocery store next to that farmer, where he goes to get his groceries.

Our planet gives us everything we need. Everything that we have comes from our planet. Our fruits and vegetables, meat, fish, wood for building homes, copper for wiring our homes, metal for making cars, cement for making concrete, sand for making glass.

Every single thing that you have, look at, and touch, comes from our planet.

Right now, everyone competes to see just how much money they can make. Why is competition so important to humans? In all competitions, there are winners and there are losers. Has society put in place any mechanisms to help the losers? No, they live under bridges, in tunnels, on the streets. They're forced to scrounge, steal, and sacrifice their self-worth just to survive. Our fellow man that we are connected to, is literally discarded.

§

Based on a 2015 report, it is estimated that in the United States on any given night, you will find 564,708 people homeless with nearly 23% of them being children.[24] Worldwide, that number is 100 million and as many as 1 billion people lack adequate housing (based on a 2005 survey by the UN).

§

## The Great Depression

To highlight the absurdity of money and its existence, we need look no further than the Great Depression.

The Great Depression was a worldwide economic depression that spanned many countries starting around 1929 and lasting until the late 1930's. Street vendors were selling apples for a nickel. There were soup kitchens everywhere. The term "skid row" was coined. So what was the issue?

It started after a fall in stock prices beginning in September 1929 and spread worldwide with the stock market crash of October 29, 1929. As a consequence, people lost their jobs. Unemployment in the United States reached a high of 25% in 1933. As a result, people had no money to buy food. So let's be clear, the issue was a lack of money, not a lack of food.

Yes, there was a drought in the U.S. at one point during this time period, but generally that wasn't the issue. Food was abundant and available (or would have been available) just as it was before the depression started. The oceans were still full of fish, cows were still plentiful in pastures, and chickens roamed free in farms throughout the country. So were raw materials such as trees, coal, and iron still plentiful. The earth did not stop giving away all its richness during that time.

§

But because people had no money to pay the wealthy, the person that stood between them and food, they couldn't eat. Think of the absurdity of having hungry Americans or anyone for that matter not being allowed to eat food that was there, available to eat.

What happened to all that food at the time? Where did it go? We know it existed before the depression took hold. So who ate it? What about the perishable foods? Did it just go to waste?

Once the depression took hold, farmers stopped producing food and some abandoned their farms. There was an absolute ripple effect. This ripple effect was the result of one thing and one thing only, money. Had there not been the existence of money, acting as the middleman, then Americans would not have gone through such hard times. The Great Depression wasn't about a lack of resources, it was about money.

This is a clear example of money controlling humanity and its destiny and not the other way around. It wasn't until we entered WWII in 1941 that the United States came out of the Great Depression. Yes, war was the reason that our economy flourished. Is it any surprise that war and money are connected to each other? Two evils allowed to co-exist in our world.

§

The system we have now in which the wealthy greatly benefit is inherently flawed. If the wealthy could somehow get what they want which is to get rid of all the poor people, all the starving people, all the elderly people collecting Social Security, and all those on social programs such welfare and food stamps, just get rid of them all—after all, according to them, these people are not contributing anything to society, that they are a drain on the economy. And when they say that, they're basically saying that these people are not buying any of their goods or services, so they are not contributing to that person's wealth, so in essence, "what good are they?"

And let's say that the wealthy were successful in doing that, ridding the entire world of the poor. The problem would be that by the very nature of the system we have, they would end up creating a new breed of poor people. This is because the system is based on competition, which means that there would be winners and losers. So, some of those wealthy individuals would lose their money and become poor. The system itself would breed classes from the very rich to the very poor. It would have to in order to support the wealthy. After all, who's going to be the chauffeur, or clean their bathrooms, mow their lawns, clean sewer lines, etc.? So you see, this system is inherently flawed.

§

When I say "system," I'm referring to any system (political or financial) you can think of that ends with "ism" and uses currency in its implementation: for example, capitalism, socialism, communism, fascism, etc. All these "ism's" are flawed and will be unsustainable in the very near future. And while this may appear to sound like some form of "ism" such as socialism, you would be correct *if* that was the only change being advocated. But when taken in combination with all the other solutions set forth in this book, you have the makings of a brand-new system designed to benefit every single person on this planet.

It takes into consideration not just what a person needs to physically survive in this world (food, water, shelter, etc.) but also takes into consideration a person's emotional and spiritual needs as well. It's no longer choosing between your survival and your soul.

It no longer requires giving up something to get something. It allows you to have both in abundance. This is the next step in our evolution.

$$\oint$$

Some people may say that if a person doesn't have to work for money, then they won't work at all. This simply isn't true. People will still work even if they don't have to, or don't need to. Those who love their jobs will still do their jobs. Doctors will still heal the sick and janitors will still clean bathrooms. Because I believe it is in our nature as human beings to want, to need to do our part, especially if we are no longer under pressure and under stress to do it.

And even if that were partly true, that some wouldn't work, that's okay, because the best part is that there will be virtually an endless supply of labor available to fill just about any job opening instantly. In the blink of an eye, you would have a labor supply of 7.7 billion people (minus the elderly and children of course).

§

People want to feel as if they are contributing to and belonging. And by taking money out of the equation, you have removed competition and the stress of making ends meet. You give people freedom—freedom to choose, to do the right thing. You give them joy, time with their family and time to enrich one's soul.

Let us abandon money and the power to control others because when you think about it, isn't that the only purpose of money?

§

# Chapter 11
# Population Control

## Solution Two

We can't talk about ending the use of money without talking about the planet's population, or by first talking about the planet itself.

Consider this: Our planet spins on its axis at a speed of 1037 miles per hour. While it's doing that, it's also moving around the sun, hurdling through space at 67,000 miles per hour. And while that's happening, the sun (and us as well) is also moving around our galaxy, the center of the Milky Way at 483,000 miles per hour. Finally, the Milky Way (along with everything contained in it) is also moving through space at 1.3 million miles per hour.[25]

We are but a mere speck of dust in the vastness of this universe.

§

And in this ever-expanding universe, there is only one place that we can call home. Our very existence is rooted in *only* this planet; a planet with a defined set of limits. If you got on a plane and headed east or west, north or south, and just kept flying, you would end up back where you started. At the equator, the circumference of our planet is 24,902 miles. From the North Pole to the South Pole, the circumference is 24,860 miles. At the 45th parallel line (approx. half way between the equator and North Pole, the circumference is only 17,588 miles. For example, if you lived in Minneapolis, Minnesota, and flew out east or west, you would only fly 17,588 miles before you ended up where you started.

The earth is made up of 71% water, which means that there's only 29% land. If we were to take the 29% of land we have and formed a planet (excluding all the water), then our new planet would have a circumference of just 7,222 miles at the equator and flying out of Minneapolis, you would only fly 5,100 miles before you found yourself back home.

If you factor in parts of the planet that are uninhabitable due to extreme temperatures, mountainous conditions, etc., what you're left with is an even smaller portion of just how much land is available for man to live on. What seems then to be a really big planet, is actually not.

Everything in the universe has a limit, a number attached to it. Water has a freezing point of 32F and a boiling point of 212F. Iron melts at 2800F. Light travels at 186,000 miles per second. A black hole has a tipping point in where once you reach that edge, nothing can escape its pull, not even light.

We tend to think of ourselves as somehow superior beings, but when you think about the magnitude of this universe, we are merely tiny creatures occupying a very small space in it. The trouble is our ego won't let us see the true reality of our existence.

§

## Cockroaches — 300 Million Years Old and Going Strong

These marvelous creatures (not the ones found in your home) have been around since the dinosaurs. Cockroaches occupy a space within our space. They produce offspring with reckless abandon, without considering whether it's beneficial to do so or not. They just do it. As a species, as a group, do we think about whether we should produce more offspring to inhabit our planet? As a group, we do not. We feel that it's a personal choice, and no one else's business, but I would like to challenge that view.

§

When you look at population growth and how we are increasing our population at a rate of 1 billion people every 15 years, you'd think that a race is going on. A race to see who's going to get to the finish line first. And just like in a race, competition is present again. You are in a competition with your fellow man to see whether your genes (your blood line) can continue, no matter what the consequences are.

While this desire to continue our bloodline is so strong in humans, have you ever stopped to ask yourself some practical questions? Like why do I have this consuming need to produce offspring? Why is it that *my* genes need to live on? Do I offer something special in my genes that will help the world? And if I feel this way, and others feel the same way, then no one will stop reproducing.

*"I'm not going to give any thought to why I shouldn't have any children, let the government, let our planet figure it out. Let my son/daughter figure it out when they get old. I'm just going to have my child(ren), raise them, and I will consider that as having done my job."*

§

But what are the implications of everyone thinking this way? Of just giving in to our natural instinct to reproduce? In that respect, we are no different from a cockroach. Cockroaches are driven by a natural instinct to reproduce. They don't think about the implications, such as how producing offspring could affect the resources that are available: food, water, trees, shelter, air quality, nor the impact on other organisms, animals, or the ecological implications, the increased competition among each other, the effects on behavior, the fight for survival, and the pressures to survive.

But the difference is that cockroaches don't need to consider those things because their size, life expectancy, and impact (footprint) on this planet is negligible. Ours is not.

§

It may surprise you to know that these 300 million-year-old species have an egalitarian and democratic society. Yes, it's true. Cockroaches survived a mass extinction some 65 million years ago that brought about the demise of dinosaurs and 70% of all life. Is it a coincidence that through its challenging evolution, that this species, through natural selection, adopted an egalitarian and democratic arrangement as its most efficient and wisest course for its survival? Can we learn from these amazing creatures that have been around for hundreds of millions of years and have chosen egalitarianism as the most efficient, logical course for their survival?

The German and American cockroaches have an elaborate social structure that could surpass some of us humans. According to Lihoreau, Costa, and Rivault, "The social biology of domiciliary cockroaches...can be characterized by a common shelter, overlapping generations, non-closure of groups, equal reproductive potential of group members, an absence of task specialization, high levels of social dependence, central place foraging, social information transfer, kin recognition, and a meta-population structure."[26]

Their research shows that group-based decision-making is responsible for complex behaviors such as resource allocation. For example, in a study, 50 cockroaches were placed in a dish with three shelters, each capable of holding only 40 cockroaches. The cockroaches arranged themselves in two shelters with 25 insects in each, leaving the third shelter empty.

When you think about, it's pretty remarkable how they cooperated to split themselves up perfectly at 25 per each shelter, not 26 in one and 24 in the other. There was no fighting, no arguing, just peacefully cooperating with each other as an entire group.

They go on to say that when the capacity of the shelters were increased to more than 50 insects, all the cockroaches arranged themselves in one shelter. Cooperation and competition are balanced in group decision-making behavior.

Do we as humans balance cooperation and competition? Do we participate in group-making decisions that affect the lives of billions of people? Of course not, group-making decisions does not exist, only competition.

We place the lives of billions of people in the hands of a few "leaders" to do whatever they want with them.

§

In some ways, a cockroach exhibits positive human-like traits that seem to be disappearing in humans.

Traits like "non-closure of groups" which means that should a cockroach come wandering in from another group, they are welcomed.

Or "an absence of task specialization" which means there is no work that would be considered beneath them.

Or "high level of social dependence." "Cockroaches do not like to be left alone and suffer ill health when they are. And they form closely bonded, egalitarian societies, based on social structures and rules."[27]

Our social component with one another is more about competition and less about cooperation. Our decision-making is about our self-interest and little to zero about anyone else's.

§

What's amazing is that when the cockroaches were given an opportunity to live in three shelters, they opted to live in only two. Had we been those cockroaches, I can without a doubt see one of the wealthy cockroaches leaving all the others behind to live in that 3rd shelter all alone, probably in a very desirable neighborhood with a gate in the front.

§

There is one thing however that distinguishes us from a cockroach and that is the impact that each birth has on our planet and on the rest of society. Just how much food is consumed during a person's lifetime, how much waste is produced? How much fossil fuel is burnt by that person in keeping his/her home brightly lit and heated or in traveling to work? How many more animals will be displaced or become extinct as world population grows and we continue to expand our presence and strip the planet at an alarming rate of natural resources? What about the quality of the air, the quality of the water, the quality of the food?

Producing offspring without giving any thought to these issues is reckless. More so, why is it an individual choice? Why can't we as a member of the group get a say in this?

In the United States, there is very little attention given to scientists who are sounding the alarm bells on this problem. How many people can this planet handle?

When you get into an elevator, there's a sign stating the maximum occupancy. Every confined space has a limit. Our planet is a confined space and so far, there's no other planet we could move to when this one gets full. Scientists can factor in the amount of fish we have in the ocean that we can safely hunt, the amount of pollution we are causing, the amount of waste we are producing, the amount of land we are destroying, the wildlife species we can safely make extinct, but they can't tell us how many human beings this planet can handle at any one time?

§

It's appalling when you think about population growth in these terms: destruction of entire ecological systems by decimating hundreds of year old trees in the tens of thousands of acres and along with it thousands of species that all become extinct just so some man somewhere can collect pieces of paper to put in the bank. All so we can keep up with this rampant outbreak of producing offspring.

§

As the planet continues to get more and more crowded, there will be greater competition for resources among neighbors and among countries. Why follow this path? A path filled with animosity, hatred, violence and despicable acts all so each person can try to carry their bloodline to the next generation.

Why? What does it mean to you after you've lived your life and are now gone?

§

Having offspring without giving any thought as to the consequences, just so you can carry your genes into the next generation, is a selfish act that is causing harm to your fellow man.

Shouldn't we as a group take care of those living with us first before considering reproduction?

Shouldn't we take care of the starving children, the homeless families in our neighborhood first? Or as a society, have we decided that we are going to have a group of "disposable people?" People without value that mean absolutely nothing to us because they don't have our genes or because they don't have any money.

We are all one group, and no matter the differences and distances between us, the decision to increase our world population should be made by the group.

# Chapter 12
# No More Countries

## Solution Three

It was only 335 million years ago that our planet had just one body of land. One supercontinent called Pangaea. Imagine if this one supercontinent never separated into what we have today. We would either be in a constant state of perpetual wars or it's more likely after all the wars have been fought and won, that by now, we would all be at peace, united under one country. And what would this country be? In essence, it would be a country that represents the entire world. And if that's the case, then you could do away with the word "country."

A country defines its borders; it creates a distinctive flag; it creates a patriotic song for you to sing, and it dresses you in a certain manner. It lets you believe that you are different from your enemy, from other countries. That you are somehow special, a child of God perhaps, and it paints your enemy as non-human, an alien, not connected to you in any way; an outside force that wants to destroy you. For the more aggressive countries, it concocts a reason for you to believe this so you will willingly go off to fight your so-called enemies. It taps into your feelings of fear and gives you reasons why you should hate.

**The impact of the wealthy and powerful acting under the flag of their country, exercising power and control over their citizens under the guise that they are doing so for the benefit of their people has been the greatest fraud humanity has ever witnessed. Our history books are filled with such people.**

§

The Gulf War is an example of this. On August 2, 1990, Saddam Hussein, Iraq President at the time, ordered the invasion of his troops into Kuwait. Why did he do it? Money of course. Saddam Hussein had incurred large amounts of debt from an eight-year war with Iran. So, a small, oil rich country such as

Kuwait made for an easy target. Because of that one decision, tens of thousands and perhaps upwards of 100,000 people lost their lives. Think about it—some innocent child sitting somewhere doing something like watching TV or playing outside in the street, minding her own business and a bomb comes crashing down, ending her life. Or a young man that just turned 18 with no job prospects joins the Iraqi Army or the United States Army to make a life for himself and before he realizes what's happening, he is in a war and is now dead. All because of one man full of ego, hatred, greed, and unable or unwilling to control those evil notions that live within his heart. One decision by one wealthy, powerful individual and a hundred thousand people lose their lives. Just like that.

§

Hitler is another example. One man responsible for at least 40 million deaths; many of which were not quick and painless. The Nazis conducted gruesome experiments such as breaking bones repeatedly in the same place to see how many times it could be done before a bone would no longer heal. Or hitting someone's head with a hammer to determine what force it would take before a skull broke open. Or amputating limbs needlessly to perform transplantations.

Imagine the hatred that must exist in a person's heart to do those things to another human being. Could you see yourself torturing your pet? Breaking its leg over and over again? Would you be able to see it in constant pain, suffering at your hands? Of course not. The thought alone probably makes you sick to your stomach.

So how did a man such as Hitler rise to power? Two reasons have been attributed. The first is the defeat in WWI some 15 years prior, which many Germans saw as humiliating (damaging to the ego). The second was the economic depression of the 1930s that hit Germany hard, causing a 30% unemployment rate (money).

Hitler came along promising people who were desperate for change, a better more prosperous life, and a new glorious Germany. And so, with the Nationalist party winning the majority of the vote, Hitler is appointed Reich Chancellor and the rest is history.

When governments, leaders, and powerful individuals place their people in desperate situations (for example, people can't afford to eat), the outcome will invariably be an extreme swing of actions in the opposite direction. It is a predictable outcome.

§

Imagine a slow-moving pendulum. As the pendulum is moving in one direction, current negative events begin to develop, such as high unemployment, wounded pride about past events, hunger, and a lack of adequate resources. Those negative events cause the pendulum to slow down on its up swing towards the apex. Now introduce an outside charismatic force to act upon that pendulum. Aided by gravity (resentment, hatred, fear by the people), it doesn't take much for this outside force to stop the direction of that pendulum and begin to reverse its swing.

The force and speed with which the pendulum swings back is directly linked to where the pendulum was in relation to the apex. If the pendulum was at the apex or near the apex, then you get a forceful quick swing back in the opposite direction. As it starts to swing back and crosses past the halfway mark, it enters the point of no return. That is, it becomes impossible to stop and reverse its direction until it reaches the end of its swing. By that time, it's too late. Whatever monster the citizens of that country have put in power, they can no longer stop.

§

It's not a coincidence that WWII began during the Great Depression. I'm sure we've all heard the phrase "Desperate times call for desperate measures." When the world, and nearly all countries in the world, face unemployment of horrific proportions, when people have no food or job, and someone comes along, monster or no monster, and says to his countrymen that he hears you and that he has a plan to restore your pride, create jobs, and put food on your table, he becomes a powerful force. The people of that country will grant this person anything and everything he wants to do, so long as he takes care of them.

§

The outcome of these pendulum swings have resulted in war killings of nearly 500 million (500,000,000) people in the last 2000 years. Wars of man killing man. Half a billion-people killed, or should I say murdered, by other people. Ordered by someone to do it.

Commanded by egotistical, maniacal, delusional, crazed, power hungry, ruthless hate-filled hearts, with justifications given in abundance to hide the horrors that were undertaken. Once the pendulum begins to swing in that direction, there's nothing that can stop it until it reaches the apex (except of course another outside force).

§

**We've allowed our rulers their egos, often stoking them in a gracious manner out of fear, respect, or some crazy notion that they are somehow superior to us. And we give what little power we have (that being our acceptance) away so freely to the wealthy and powerful. That becomes our price of wanting and needing to be a part of that country, of depending on the wealthy and powerful to take care of us.**

That is our history!

Should the past continue to define us? Should our past keep us in a box with no opportunity to expand beyond what was and what is? What about what **could be**?

§

Imagine a world with no countries—none that would link you to an artificial idea created by man in an effort to elicit loyalty out of you. Loyalty so that you might fight other men and die if called upon. B*ut loyalty to whom?* **Loyalty to those who have power and control: Loyalty to the wealthy of course.** Have you ever seen a poor person, a homeless person for example that's powerful? No, of course not. That doesn't exist in our world. Therefore, power and control go hand in hand with wealth. The terms are essentially interchangeable. If you're wealthy, then power and control over others flows to you naturally, like a river flowing into an ocean. The same cannot be said of a poor person however.

**In this new world, I honor the past. All those men and women from all the different countries that fought and died for their country, for their beliefs, I honor them all.**

But being human requires that we continually grow, continually strive to be better on the inside. Every single war that has been fought on this planet has been man versus man, not man versus alien. I'm quite certain that God doesn't want that. Certainly, God is not rooting for one team over the other. The absurdity, the audacity to think that you are on the right side and that God is with you and that God would be okay with you killing his other sons/daughters. Do you really believe that somehow God has favored you over his other children?

Think about the belief that you are special. You *are* special, but are you any *more* special than anyone else? If you say yes, then why? Is it because you're smarter, possess more money, have a nice house and a fancy car? Really? That's what you think makes you so special? Special in the eyes of God?

The hypocrisy, the justifications we employ in our heads are endless. We go through life fooling ourselves, trying to find some semblance of happiness so that we can avoid looking at ourselves in the mirror.

§

Let's end fighting for resources, for wealth, for political ideology, religious ideology, or simply ego and pride. Let's stop wishing and hoping someone does badly so you can do well. Instead of a divided world always trying to harm the other, what about a united world? Can you imagine what astonishing accomplishments this world would have with 7.7 billion people all working together?

§

Don't you think that with billions of people working together, we could all unite to physically build families homes so that no one is homeless, to physically grow more food so no one starves? Of course, we can.

We can create a world where each of us finds fulfillment by helping one another! When we don't have to worry about our survival, about where our next meal is coming from, or worry about making money, you would be surprised how amazing we are as human beings. How giving and loving we can be.

Evil does not want us to know that part of ourselves. But our existence, our purpose, has always been to help our fellow man. And by doing so, by giving happiness to someone else, you get to keep your heart and your soul alive and you get to take it with you.

And if you are incapable of helping your fellow man, that's okay too. But you should at the very least not hurt your fellow man. That should not be your purpose in life.

§

It all starts with a simple concept: a fundamental belief that we are all equal. The minute you start to think that you are better than anyone else, all hope is lost. Can you do that? Can you see that other people's lives are as valuable as your own? That their death is equivalent to your death?

§

As populations in each country grow and as world resources begin to dwindle, what you'll find is countries fighting to get those resources for their people. In short, countries will turn into gangs: street gangs with turfs and boundaries, invading other turfs to steal their resources or to increase the size of their turf.

## The Whole is Greater than the Sum of its Parts

Aristotle once said, "The whole is greater than the sum of its parts." The brilliance of Aristotle captures something that is so powerful and yet so elusive. The reason it's so elusive is because it's not apparent to the naked eye. Nor is it mathematically logical. That is the reason why it's rarely believed or understood.

1+1+1+1=9.

We look at this mathematical equation frowning and smirking. It's not correct, not right, how can that be? But the answer 9 is correct. Not mathematically of course, but in this context.

Take a piece of rope. Rope is comprised of a group of strands of yarn twisted together. If we measured the tensile strength of each strand of yarn in that rope, we would find for example, that each strand could handle 10 pounds of weight before it breaks. If we had 6 of those strands, then we could say that those 6 strands could hold 60 pounds of weight. But if we took those 6 strands and put them together, they would be able to hold not just 60 pounds, but 150 pounds of weight before they broke.

How can that be? It's because the whole is truly greater than the sum of its parts.

Businesses also understand that concept and call it "synergy." So much more can be accomplished when people work together towards a common goal than when we all do it apart. Imagine all the countries on this planet working together to produce energy, food, minerals, and sharing all those resources. You would have an abundance of everything. You would produce more of everything. Poverty, homelessness, starvation, a lack of adequate water and energy—all of it would disappear. Crime, education, health, climate change and so much more including most of our social issues would practically disappear or vastly improve.

§

The wealthy and powerful would, no doubt, dispute this notion. They would tell you that it's a fantasy, that it's not possible. They've always said the same thing about people starving; that the planet simply doesn't have resources to feed everyone. But this is a blatant myth. World population grew from 1 billion in 1850 to 7.7 billion in present day. And somehow, we've managed to feed all those people year after year. Somehow, we've managed to meet all that demand for water, shelter, and food.

So, if all the countries united, we would end an era in human history marked by plight, hatred, pain, suffering, and enter a new era of compassion and caring.

There's just one thing standing in the way of this idea: the wealthy and powerful. The "middlemen" if you will. Egos abound, and hatred at the ready to fire. Ready to squash such notions.

§

# Chapter 13
# The Final Chapter in Our History

## What It Costs You to Hate

Hate has a price tag—it's not free. It is detrimental to your health, to your soul, and to the kind of life you want to live. But many of us have made hate a need in our lives. Just as we need food and water, a lot of us have made hate a necessary nourishment that we must consume on a regular basis. Hatred and anger offer so much comfort to us and we are so used to them that they've become our best friends. We call on them often when we feel the world is unfair and when we are in so much pain.

It becomes very easy for hatred to enter the heart when we feel that we are being treated unfairly and are powerless to change our situation. Much of the unfairness we feel is about money. Whether it's because of a job or no job, wages being low, not being able to afford to buy something, envy—it's almost always about money.

If we correlated the rise in hatred of our fellow man with the growing income disparity that exists today, we would find a direct connection. In other words, the bigger the financial gap between the wealthy and poor/middle-class, the more people will feel hate and the stronger that hate will be.

While I don't believe that the wealthy and powerful intended for this rise and degree of hate in our society, I do believe that now that it's here, they welcome it. Why? Because they are able to channel the hate people feel away from them and towards something else. With smoke coming out of our ears, we are clouded from seeing the truth.

**The truth being that the income disparity, the unfair treatment of the wealthy towards the poor/middle-class is directly attributable to them and only to them and not to some scapegoat group.**

❨

And once *hate* has entered the heart, it does not want to leave. If you've ever really tried to kick *hate* out of your heart, you know that it fights you every step of the way. It kicks and screams, it fills your head with all sorts of justifications of why it should stay. It becomes its own entity that is not you, but that lives inside you.

❨

Sometimes we find ourselves hating people and we don't even know why. Sometimes, we stop listening to *hate* and listen to the person or group we hate and get a real awakening. That all this time, *hate* has been lying to us.

But some of us feel it's okay to hurt others so that we may benefit, so that we may have a better life.

These individuals don't understand that we are all connected. The dream, vision or whatever you want to call it that I had, proved that to me. We are all connected on a tangible, physical level. I know it may sound crazy. But let me ask you this, if you experienced the same vision that I experienced, would you behave any differently?

Understand that those who pretend to be superior to you are not. They probably know less than you do. Don't let them manipulate you by tapping into your fears or hatred, because when you let them, they gain control over you. It's like a ventriloquist sticking his hand into his puppet. And once they've gotten their hand up your back, they gain control over you, and you end up doing things that quite literally hurts your own self-interest and those of your family.

So how can you extinguish the *hate* that lives inside of you? First understand that the *hate* that is present in you is manmade. You weren't born with that feeling in your heart. You weren't and you know it. A newly born child doesn't have hate.

It's manmade by evil that understands you better than you understand yourself: Manmade by individuals who have used trickery to get you to hate a group or groups of people who are innocent and probably face the same problems that you do.

Why have these evil people done this to you? Money and power, plain and simple. Is there anything else greater in this world for those people? The answer is NO. Controlling someone is the ultimate form of power on our planet. There is nothing greater. Think about it. I challenge you to come up with something greater. You'll find that none exists. Nuclear weapons, armies, anything you can think of is designed for one thing and one thing only—to control: to control a group, a country, a person; to get them to behave a certain way or do a certain thing or face the ultimate form of control. The ability to control your existence— that is whether to let you live or die.

§

## Is God to Blame?

We are all God's children, yet some of us forget that. Some of us feel that we are above being God's children, perhaps even above God himself. Much like Lucifer felt that he could be God and wanted to be God, some of us are full of those same notions of superiority, and are incapable of controlling our ego.

And just as some of us feel hatred towards others, there are those that feel hatred towards God himself. Some people blame God for their predicament or when something tragic happens such as an innocent child born with a genetic abnormality or getting cancer or a car accident. After all, if God exists and is so great, then why is he allowing all of this to occur?

But what if God had absolutely nothing to do with those tragic events? We wanted God to stay out of our way. We wanted free will. Well, the genetic abnormality of that child is just that, an abnormality as a consequence of our genetic makeup as human beings. Or in the case of someone with cancer, a result of environment or genes. Or in the case of a car accident, a result of happenstance.

The point is we can't have it both ways. We can't ask God to interfere when it's of benefit and the rest of the time to stay out of our way. He isn't some genie in a bottle we call upon as it suits us. In addition, if God were to intervene in your life to help you, then he would also be interfering/controlling the free will of someone else. For example, if you begged God to not let the bank foreclose on your home and God were to somehow help you, then God would be interfering with the lives and free will of the owners of the bank as well as the couple that end up buying your foreclosed home. And since God sees us as equal to each other, he's not going to give you preference over his other children.

There is no way for God to help you without controlling/intervening with the free will of someone else or altering the course of humanity. Every single action, every single event, has or will have some impact on someone else. That is a fact. You may not be able to see the impact of your actions and it may not even occur during your lifetime, but it will happen. There is no escaping that.

So, with the understanding that you might feel anger and hatred, I'm going to ask you anyway: **give up hatred of your fellow man**. Whether you hate your fellow man because of his skin color, ethnicity, social status, or whatever it is, just give it up. You don't need to feel this way. Allow your fellow man to be equal to you because he/she is.

§

What I've offered you here is an end to the pain and unfairness you feel. If you don't want life to treat you unfairly, then you can't treat others unfairly or accept unfair situations on someone else. If you don't want to feel pain, then you can't cause pain to someone else or let pain happen to someone else.

## The Choice We Face

*I can't be happy if you are sad. I can't enjoy my life if you are suffering.*

What kind of a life is it when we make ourselves numb to all the misery that we see just so we can be happy? When we toss our hands up in the air and say, "That's just the way it is. There's nothing we can do about it."

There is something we can do about it and time is fast approaching when all of us will be forced to make a decision.

1. The wealthy and powerful will need to decide whether they will let the rest of us share in the planet's resources or if they will keep it all for themselves? Right now, one percent of the population owns 50% of the total wealth. What

will it be five years from now, ten years from? Will it be 60%, 70%, 80%? Will they, on their own, ever say that they are taking too much of the pie? Will their morality, decency, or even their humanity ever guide them? Or will they simply turn their back on us?

2. Law enforcement will need to decide whether it will side with the citizens it swore to protect or side with money and power? Having actual physical power to control the masses, will they abandon us in favor of their own self-interest or will they rise to the occasion and see their role as the protectors of humanity?

3. And the rest of us will also need to decide if hatred and anger will win out resulting in us turning on each other in order to survive? Or can we somehow come together as group leaving all our negative emotions at the door in an effort to **think clearly** so that we can make practical, logical decisions designed to benefit every single person on this planet?

∫

The solutions presented in this book, I believe, are the only **peaceful** means to saving humanity. **And they must all be done.** We must end the use of money, unite all the countries as one and control our population. Those three simple solutions, while difficult to implement, will result in peace, and ensure the survival of our souls.

**If we are successful, you will find man's love, compassion and soul grow exponentially with each passing day. It will be the most amazing transformation of any species to date. We will also be able to save our planet, save other creatures from extinction, and operate with amazing efficiency and innovation, as there will be collaboration on everything (from health and medicine to science and technology) throughout the world.**

$$\int$$

There is a real opportunity here to turn earth into Heaven; Heaven on earth. Have you seen all the beauty and wonder of this planet we call our home? The 400,000 species of plants or the nearly 8 million species of animals that live among us. Have you seen the vast oceans, majestic mountains, forests, and meadows?

God gave us the most amazing planet any species could hope for—a planet so diverse and awe-inspiring. And the reason I say, "God gave us" is because we are the only creatures on this planet that can truly appreciate it all. A lion, a tiger, a bear, all have small worlds and are confined to those worlds. We have the ability to see so many small worlds within our planet and appreciate them all.

He also gave us a soul, the ultimate sustaining entity that exists in each and every one of us.

§

## Interconnectedness

In the afterlife, interconnectedness and joy is what we have; it's who we are as a species. There are no divisions among religions, ethnicities, nationalities, color, or anything else. Hatred doesn't exist either.

Interconnectedness is the reason we *have to* be this way. It's the reason why we *have to* look out for each other, protect each other, love each other. Because interconnectedness is real; it's not manmade; it's not a gimmick; it exists.

And so there it is, the answer intently looking at us, staring us right in the face, but we are too blinded, too brainwashed, too egotistical to see it. This is what I believe God has creeded:

**That our world will either be Heaven for everyone or Heaven for no one.**

Again…

**Heaven for Everyone or Heaven for No One.**

§

And that is because of interconnectedness. Our souls are not just joined together in the afterlife, they are joined together now, in this life. As a result, since we are connected to one another now, it becomes impossible for one person to have heaven on earth while others suffer. The universe, this planet, our nature, and our souls will not allow this fundamental law to be broken. We can keep ignoring this fundamental law. We can keep trying to fit a square peg in a round hole, but it will never work. We can keep trying to let a few among us be happy while others suffer, but this law will never allow it to succeed.

This creed and this fundamental law of interconnectedness that I've stated, I believe exists not by chance, but by design. It was made this way on purpose. Why do you suppose?

§

In the thousands of years that we have existed, we have lived our lives as if we weren't connected. We have fought each other, killed each other and hated each other in a desperate attempt to extinguish the one trait we have—our ability to love.

I ask you, do our history books portray a "Heaven on earth?" No, not even close.

There's only one logical conclusion to be drawn then; the intent for our existence is to learn, to master what it means to be human. What it means to have a soul.

And if we are successful, then and only then is heaven on earth possible.

If you can believe that in the afterlife our souls are bound to one another with nothing but pure love emanating from us, then you can believe that we have it within us right now; that we don't acquire our souls after we die; that our souls exist within us now. And if that's the case, then it's just a matter of choice.

Choose. Choose to believe that we ALL have souls. Choose to believe that we are ALL connected to each other.

Just as God could have controlled Lucifer and made him nice, He didn't. He let Lucifer be what he wanted. You have free will. What will you choose?

I hope you will choose love. I hope you will choose to create heaven on earth.

And so, this is the solution to the puzzle that faces us today. This is what will save humanity. This is what will preserve our souls.

I want everyone reading this book to understand that you have worth. Your worth isn't based on how much money you have or what your status is in society.

Your worth comes from the fact that you exist in our group, the group of human beings; that your soul is extremely valuable, as valuable as everyone else's.

Let's usher in a new era where your right to exist and live a happy life is guaranteed no matter where you live on this planet. That this right exists by virtue of having a soul. Where your true purpose isn't about your needs and your desire to continue your genes, but about helping others and enriching your soul, the one thing, the only thing you will be able to take with you.

Heaven on earth is only possible if it exists for everyone. Period. No exceptions. Not even a single exception.

❡

# *References*

[1] Lyudmila Trut, Early Canid Domestication: The Farm-Fox Experiment, American Scientist (Volume 87, March-April 1999).

[2] Julia Lindberg et al., Selection for tameness has changed brain gene expression in silver foxes, Current Biology (Volume 15 Issue 22, November 2005).

[3] I don't know what the concept of killing someone who doesn't exist in our reality would be, but it would be reasonable to say that if God is omnipotent as most of us believe and therefore more powerful than Lucifer, an Archangel, then there must exist some form of death or of ceasing to exist and that God would have such a power. God also has other choices such as taking Lucifer's free will, as well as altering his behavior and making him good.

[4] Source: FBI.

[5] Lynn Langton, Marcus Berzofsky, Christopher Krebs, Hope Smiley-McDonald, Victimizations Not Reported to the Police, 2006 – 2010, Bureau of Justice Statistics, U.S. Department of Justice, August 2012.

[6] Source: FBI.

[7] David Griffith, The 2016 POLICE Presidential Poll, POLICE Magazine, September 2, 2016.

[8] As of January 25th, 2017, North Dakota has introduced a bill (House Bill 1203) that would make it legal to commit vehicular homicide if that act is perpetrated upon a protester. While the language in the bill tries to conceal that scenario, it would in fact apply if the driver were to simply state that the act committed was "unintentional" when it was not.

[9] A Super PAC is a political entity that can solicit, collect and spend an <u>unlimited</u> amount of money to get a candidate elected.

[10] Laura Shin, The 85 Richest People In The World Have As Much Wealth As The 3.5 Billion Poorest, Forbes.com, January 23, 2014.

[11] Giles Keating, Michael O'Sullivan, Anthony Shorrocks, James Davies, Rodrigo Lluberas, Credit Suisse, Global Wealth Report 2010, November 2010.

[12] Anthony Shorrocks, James Davies, Rodrigo Lluberas, Antonios Koutsoukis, Credit Suisse, Global Wealth Report 2016, November 2016.

[13] Ibid.

[14] Ibid.

[15] Laura Shin, The 85 Richest People In The World Have As Much Wealth As The 3.5 Billion Poorest, Forbes.com, January 23,2014.

[16] Emmanuel Saez, Gabriel Zucman, Wealth Inequality In The United States Since 1913:

Evidence From Capitalized Income Tax Data, Working Paper 20625, October 2014.

[17] Ibid.

[18] Ibid.

[19] Ibid.

[20] Ibid.

[21] Edward Wolff, The Asset Price Meltdown and the Wealth of the Middle Class, August 26, 2012.

[22] Emmanuel Saez, Gabriel Zucman, Wealth Inequality In The United States Since 1913: Evidence From Capitalized Income Tax Data, Working Paper 20625, October 2014.

[23] Ibid.

[24] Meghan Henry, Azim Shivji, Tanya de Sousa, Rebecca Cohen, The 2015 Annual Homeless Assessment Report (AHAR) to Congress, November 2015.

[25] Galaxies are not really moving. Instead what is believed to be happening is that the space between galaxies is expanding.

[26] Lihoreau, M.; Costa, J.T.; Rivault, C. (November 2012), The social biology of domiciliary cockroaches: colony structure, kin recognition and collective decisions. Insectes Sociaux. 59:445.

[27] Matt Walker, Why cockroaches need their friends, BBC Nature, May 2, 2012.

# A Note from the Author

There are some things in this world which I can freely admit I know nothing about. Then there are other things that I am confident of.

This life has been lived trying to comprehend our world and to broaden not only my perception, but my perspective.

My goal in writing this book is with the hope that together, we can change the world for the better.

I look forward to the day when we can ALL live on this planet with love in our hearts and peace in our souls.